The Lonely Boy

Dedication

I didn't complete this book for a very long time because of my parents and my mother in particular. I loved her very much and was proud of her. I didn't want to disparage either one of my parents in any way. My mom was an extremely kind and beautiful woman. She was probably the most honest and good person I have ever known. Her time with me on earth was short, but her love and goodness inspired me. If there is any good in Richard Scuderi it comes from her. I know she tried to give me tough love, as many parents of her generation did, and I appreciate all her efforts. I thank for her beauty and her wisdom and I look forward to the day when I see her again.

I also want to thank my partner, John Leahy, for all of his support and encouragement in writing this book.

Richard Scuderi

The Lonely Boy

Contents

The Lonely Boy

Chapter 1   In The Beginning

The first memory I have of life on earth was about August 1967. We were vacationing with my maternal grandparents for the weekend in the Catskills. I remember it was raining on that Saturday afternoon. We were sitting on a covered porch. I was next to my very pregnant mom, who was trying to tell me that I was going to have a new brother or sister. At two years old, I guess I didn't notice the change in my mom's size. I took the news in stride and was more concerned about the rain ending. I was the first baby in the family in a long time and was showered with attention.

 For the first five years of my life, we lived in a two family house with my father's parents. Nana and pop owned the house and lived on the first floor. We had the upstairs apartment. I remember feeling very safe and loved. My mom was a worrier and she was on me like white on rice. My pediatrician's office was right down the street and I guess you could say Dorothy, Dr. Krafcheck's nurse, was particularly familiar with me. I think that's why I never had any childhood diseases, chicken pox, measles, mumps, never had a chance on her watch. One day, I remember choking on a piece of potato. Mom turned me upside down over the stairs and cut it with her fingernail in my throat. It actually bled. She really had the mom instinct.

 I was a sweet and sensitive little boy. Mom once told me when Frosty the Snowman was on television near

The Lonely Boy

Christmas, I was inconsolable when the greenhouse door opened and Frosty was reduced to a little puddle on the floor. From very early on I was not built for all the sadness that life often reveals to us. My parents were pretty tough though, so I did develop coping skills and can navigate through difficult times without falling apart.

My parents were very strict. I was brought up to fear my parents, not to think of them as friends. I couldn't do anything without getting the nod of approval first. It was something that would follow me for the rest of my life.

On September 28, 1967, my mother gave birth to a baby girl. I was named Richard, after my father. Dad was always called Rick, though his real name was Enrico, which translates to Henry. The new baby girl was named Mary Anne after my mother.

As time would pass, it became evident the two women would have nothing in common other than their physical resemblance. They couldn't have been more different. I was happy to have a sister now and enjoyed the company. I remember playing together and being protective of her. I didn't mind sharing my life with a new person. I never felt neglected or left out. I loved having people around me and living with my grandparents made that possible.

My mom was a native New Yorker and grew up in Brooklyn. She had a hard time adapting to her new life in New Jersey. We drove to Brooklyn every Sunday in the early years for Sunday gravy and gallons of her precious

The Lonely Boy

New York water. We were extremely close to my mother's family.

My mother was the first of the Marino children to marry and leave the nest. My mother's family consisted of my Grandfather Paul, my Grandmother Mary and my mother's three siblings Simon, Jack and Maria. My mom's immediate family was quite dysfunctional. I remember seeing this early on. Also, my grandparents were not a good match. In fact, you could say that they really didn't like each other. They had separate bedrooms and were always quarreling.

My mom was the second child in the family. She had an older brother Simon. Simon was unusual. He had major issues that were never addressed. He was a loner who lived in the basement. He had girlfriends but never married. He didn't have a job and he relied on his parents for the rest of their lives. He was very good hearted, but today he would have probably been in some special needs program. Sonny, as he was known to the family, loved Manhattan and walked around the city taking pictures of tourists to make a buck. He kept odd hours but seemed to be content.

My mother's other brother, Jack, was a few years younger than my mother. He was a real momma's boy. I don't mean that as an insult. He remained very close to my grandmother until her last day. To this day, both sons still live at home and never left the home they grew up in. Jack was very much connected to my grandmother. She catered to his every whim. I think my grandmother overcompensated for her unhappy marriage by putting all her efforts into her children. With this dynamic in play, I never understood how my mother had the strength to walk on her own and start a new life. Her siblings never really did.

Finally, there was Maria. She was only 13 when I was born. She did eventually marry, but had a great deal of emotional problems.

With all that said, the early part of my life was filled with good memories, a lot of love and above all, a strong sense of family. I could have never imagined that as I approached my 50th birthday, all the family I loved so dearly would be completely gone from my life. The sadness and loss I feel is overwhelming and there have been days I feel I can't get out of bed. To me, the most important thing you can have in life is love, good friends and, of course, family.

As much as I am very ambitious, love and friendship are the most important things for me. Ironically, it has been those things that have given me the most challenges in my life.

Sometimes I feel like I am completely alone in this world. I see how people can be. How they don't have a sense of their own mortality as I do, and how they don't embrace the knowledge that our life here is limited and how we treat each other is all that really matters.

The Lonely Boy

My dad's family consisted of his father, Epifanio, and his mother, Santina. They were both born in Palermo, Sicily and never spoke a word of English. My father had an older brother, Joe. Joe was a difficult person. He was not good to my father when they were young and they were estranged for much of their adult lives. Joe's wife was Philomina. Phil, as they called her, was tough and very competitive. The kids used to call her Aunt Meany. I think she liked it. She was a vast contrast from my mom who was a girly girl. The two women would never connect and our families would never be close. Joe and Phil had three children, Joey, Mary Jo, and Michael.

There have been times in my adult life that I have been in the same public space with these people who share my DNA, and have the same last name. Yet, there was not even an acknowledgement of each other. I find that so sad and such a loss on all sides.

One of the reasons I finally decided to write this book was not to alienate people, but to bring them together. I find it absurd that I have no family, considering there are a number of blood relations within a 30 mile radius. What do you get from not talking to people? No one wins. All you wind up with is regret after they pass on. By then it's too late to change anything.

I have had a great deal of loss and health issues in my life. If I have learned anything, it is that you will not regret not responding to work emails. But you WILL regret the love you missed out on and the friendships you didn't see through to completion. Why can't people just embrace their differences and move forward together? If we were all the same, life would be very boring.

Mom and dad had master plan buy a piece of land and build their dream house. My parents paid rent, but saved for "the house." In 1968, my parents found a building lot in the Dewey Heights section of New Brunswick, New Jersey. The neighborhood was the finest in the area. It was named after the Dewey Mansion that was located at its entrance. It breaks my heart today to see how it went so far downhill. But back in the day, you could not get a better spot in New Brunswick.

My dad was in the Navy and traveled the world in his 20s. After his service, he went into business for himself, working as a contractor. He didn't marry until he was 32, which at the time, was considered late.

In those days, one income could suffice, so my mom stayed at home with us. My dad worked during the day and spent his nights and weekends building our house. I have vivid memories of being at the construction site. My dad built us a tire swing to keep us occupied when we were all there on weekends. I remember playing in the sand and walking around when the house was first framed. To this day, my favorite time in a construction project is when a house is first framed. There are so many possibilities.

The Lonely Boy

I think that's when I first got my true love for building and design. I was fortunate enough to have my dad help me build my own home some 30 years later. Dad worked for me in his later years until he got sick. I loved that we connected in that way, although at times he could be very challenging.

In August of 1970, the construction was complete and we moved in. My parents were way over budget and had to move themselves. I remember their mattress being in the back of dad's truck and it blowing off onto the highway. My mother was in tears and her Aunt Fannie and my grandmother sewed it shut when we got to the new house.

Mom and Dad built a beautiful, all brick, five bedroom center hall colonial. In its day, it was considered quite a large home. We moved in with bare bones: plywood floors in the living and dining room and not much furniture. In fact, it would be about another 10 years before it was fully furnished. I remember spending most of my young life in the parking lots of furniture stores looking for a compromise between my father's colonial and my mother's French provincial tastes.

They needed to hit the ground running because I was starting kindergarten two weeks later. My teacher, Mrs. Brown, was very elderly and we were all afraid of her. It was the 1970s and I was in a strict Catholic school. I went to school with all the other neighborhood boys, the Bradshaws, the Hardings, and the Lynches. In the early years there was a connection, but as we began to grow, obvious differences led me to become more of a loner. I was not good at sports and that was a big deal back then. I'm sure it was a disappointment to my parents, but my dad was not really interested in sports either. I spent most of my time in the backyard with my parents and my sister while I was young.

In my early years, I felt a very strong connection with God. I remember praying in church one day and felt God was talking directly to me. I saw a beautiful vision full of vibrant colors. The colors were like bubbles and they were very vivid and bright. It felt like I was looking into a kaleidoscope in a way. I wasn't sure what God was trying to tell me, but I was sure we were connecting and that his message was purposeful and specifically meant for me.

My connection with spirituality would lessen as I grew older but there was always a very strong inner voice that guided me through my life path for as long as I could remember. I am sometimes able to predict things before they happen. It isn't consistent however, so I could never be a psychic. I just try to subtly hint to people when I get a strong feeling that they are on a good or a bath path.

Growing up, my sister Mary Anne and I always went to the same schools. We even went to college together, but we were never close. Unlike my mother, who was very emotional, Mary Anne was cold and distant. She had no sense of family and always did what was best for her. I

The Lonely Boy

always wanted her to be more like me, but that just wasn't who she was.

In 1973, my mother became pregnant a third time. It was not planned and she was very unhappy about it. She had her boy and girl and they were in school now. She was done. Also, my mother had become increasingly obsessed with her body image and with being as thin as possible. A pregnancy would change that, especially now that she was in her 30s.

She stayed so thin during her pregnancy that when she finally told us three weeks before she gave birth, we had no idea. On August 28, 1973, my 34-year-old mother gave birth to a baby girl. They named her Jennifer. In the early 1970s, it was the name of the day. We had three Jennifers on our street that year. With the birth of our sister, our family was now complete. My mom had her tubes tied right afterwards. She didn't want any more children.

In the pictures from Jennifer's christening, mom was the thinnest woman there. Her slimness was now a constant in our lives and I feel it contributed to her early death.

After Jennifer was born, things began to change in our family. I noticed my parents fighting a great deal and I saw my mother becoming very unhappy in the marriage. Like her mother, she began to put all her energies into her children and didn't connect with her husband. In her defense, my dad could be a very frustrating man. Yet, she stayed with him even though I think she was unhappy. I am sure her dysfunctional background and the challenges I brought later made her life tougher.

I often wish I did not cause her so much worry. I was a very sweet kid and never got in trouble, but my lack of fitting in with the other kids hurt her and I am sorry for her pain. Especially, because her life was so short and at the end, the one person I felt closest to in the world was not connected to me emotionally anymore.

The 70s were a challenging time for my parents. We lost pop in July 1975 and I got my first taste of mortality. I remember the night pop died. It was raining very hard and my dad had just completed a sunroom addition on the back of our house.

In the middle of the night, my dad was called to the hospital. It was during a terrible summer lightning storm. My mom and the three of us kids were in the new sunroom watching the rain come down. Mom tried to explain to us about death. She said that the clouds were crying for pop-pop. To this day, when there is a strong summer storm, I remember those sweet moments and it takes away some of the sting of the horrible things that came in later years.

I was 10 when pop left us. I remember being in the schoolyard the following winter and seeing smoke come out of the big school chimney. I thought to myself for a moment, is that what happened to pop? What if he was cremated and that smoke was him leaving us? What happens to us when we die?

The Lonely Boy

Pop was buried and we all went to visit the grave many times. I guess I just had an early fear of death. After that day, I never let anyone I know be cremated. I even had my dog buried with a headstone. I feel we should honor someone's body, not destroy it.

After pop's death, nana needed a lot of help. We lived in the same town as nana. Uncle Joe also lived in New Jersey, but in Union County which was quite a distance away. So the burden of taking care of nana really fell on my father.

My father told me that nana had suffered with mental illness. As she got older, it got worse. Nana and pop had had separate bedrooms for a long time, but when he died, she was beside herself. I actually saw her vomit because she was so distraught.

I think the stress of having three children, a mom to take care of and an unhappy wife caused the perfect storm for problems in my parent's marriage. I also think that my mom's emotional issues got worse as she got older. I refer to it as MMI, Marino Mental Illness. Marino was her maiden name. I say that with much respect, as I suffer with it myself every day.

As a young boy, I once asked my mother, "What do you do with the bad thoughts?" She didn't even flinch. She said, "You have to block them and think of something else." She knew exactly what I was talking about, but I was too young to articulate it properly.

The Lonely Boy

It is sad that we all suffer so much in life. I have come to learn that life is about the journey, but I was not built for all the sadness. My mom had a premonition that she would die young and of cancer, and she started to prepare me for her death from the time I was very young. She would say things like she wanted her share of their estate to go directly to her children and that she wanted to be buried in a mausoleum. She wanted a closed casket and she wanted me to stay close to my father and sisters after she was gone.

Looking back at this as an adult now, I think she must have been depressed. I wish I could have helped her. She also seemed to confide in me personal information that you wouldn't normally tell a child. I think that's why I grew up so quickly and was so mature early in life. It also made me strong and gave me a sense of my own mortality.

My parents were creatures of habit and we never did anything spur of the moment. We had dinner every night on stools at the kitchen peninsula with Channel 4 news on. We had Chinese food every Saturday and we went to Brooklyn every Sunday for pasta and Sunday gravy, although back then I think we called it macaroni.

My parents were quite strict and my mother had a knack of knowing what we were doing at every moment. One incident that stands out was at Uncle Joe's house. Aunt Phil had asked me if I wanted something to eat. Instead of answering, I turned to my mother's eyes for the nod. Phil said, "I asked you, not your mother." I got a lot of kudos in the car on the way home for that move.

Mom was the boss and she was in charge. We were often not able to do things that other kids were doing. We had a strict set of rules and we were afraid of our parents and our teachers. My parents put double doors on the living room and dining room because we kids weren't allowed to go near them.

Every weekend morning my dad would open my curtains and say, "Rise and shine!" We weren't kids that had our own voices. I often work with young families today in my design business. The parents are always so concerned about making the house kid friendly. I want to scream every time I hear that!!! It's just so different from the way I was raised. Growing up, I could never put up a poster or do what I wanted with my room unless it was approved first. Unlike the sense of entitlement I see in many children today, from very early on, I got the message that I was a guest in my parents' home. I feel kids are like sponges. They're always looking for someone to show them the way. You need discipline in your early life to give you standards, and I've noticed that kids who grow up without it have a harder time later on in life.

Don't get me wrong, we had problems, big problems, but I will say that the discipline I received made me ambitious. I knew I couldn't count on anyone. I was going to have to be strong and figure it out myself. I was also never allowed

The Lonely Boy

to stay over or go inside any of my friend's houses. I was taught to be respectful to all adults and that children should be seen and not heard.

I decided pretty early on that I didn't want children myself. I don't think I have completely healed from my own childhood. I have learned that children come through us, but they are not us. They are their own recycled souls and come to us with a list of their own challenges and strengths. I'm afraid I would resent the fact that my children could live in a time when they can be whoever they want to be, when I was not allowed to do the same. I think of my childhood with great sadness and don't want to put that on someone else.

Growing up is hard, but growing up as a kid who doesn't fit in is awful. You feel lonely because you are not included in things that other people are included in. You also understand that your parents know and are disappointed in you. You feel like you're caught between a rock and a hard place and you don't have the maturity or skills to deal with it yet.

One of the reasons I think that I am successful in my business is that I'm able to take circumstances that are not so favorable and find ways to change them and make them more appealing. My life has been a lot like that. I have constantly been put in situations that are less than favorable and have had to find ways to put a positive spin on it and make it better. There are so many things I wish I could

The Lonely Boy

have changed in my early life. I wish I was better at sports. I wish I connected better with my peers. I wish I wasn't a worry to my parents. But for whatever reason, that isn't the way things turned out. I believe that we are put here on earth for a reason. It's your karma, if you will. This Richard Scuderi life has been a constant struggle for me with depression and anxiety. I am not sure why this is my fate, maybe to make up for sins of a past life. Maybe I needed to suffer in my early years so that I would become more compassionate to others later on. Maybe that is the gift in all of this. It is the pain that makes us better, stronger and more compassionate. Maybe that was why my destiny this time around was to be a lost and lonely boy.

The Lonely Boy

Chapter 2   The Ugly Truth

Of all the chapters in the story of my life, this is the one I struggled with the most. I even finished the book and went back and included this chapter later. I think if you're going to tell your life story, you have to be completely transparent. For me, my self esteem, or lack thereof, formed who I was then and who I am today. I would be less than honest it I didn't talk about it.

My mom was a very fearful person and I learned that when she was about to give birth to me, she was terrified. My dad had to coach her throughout. It was a long labor and a difficult birth, even though I arrived a week early. It was probably the only time in my life that I was ever early!!! My mom's journal revealed that when I was a newborn, I was very funny looking. I had a full head of straight black hair that stood up all over like Rod Stewart. I changed very quickly and by my first birthday, mom said I was the prettiest baby she had ever seen. I looked very different than the rest of my family. I had blonde hair and blue eyes. I looked more Scandinavian than Italian. People used to tease my dad about who my father really was. They would often say to me, "I think your father was really the milkman." I had soft features, was fair, and had an oval head while the rest of my family had round heads. However I think the forceps and my mom's general reluctance may have had something to do with that.

The Lonely Boy

Mom would dress me very preppy and my signature look was a bow tie and overalls. I was very sweet and could perform on command. When she took me out, I was showered with attention, much more attention than my sister got. Mom said I was the favorite. Nana would buy me the best gifts while Mary Anne got junk.

When I started in school, I was a really cute kid. In my first grade picture, I had the honor of holding the class sign. When the photographer was setting us up, he initially had another boy holding the sign. He looked into the camera and then asked me, "the blonde young man," to switch and move up front. I remember feeling special because of it even back then. I remember Mrs. Bradshaw saying my hair looked like spun gold. I was a cute little boy.

As I made the transition to tween, I received a present from the nose fairy. Like most kids I became awkward as I approached puberty, but my thin frame and ethnic nose became quite obvious. Kids at this age have no filters and this got noticed. I remember being called "The Nose" once in grammar school. In 8th grade, Regina Crea looked at me and said, "I think you're really good looking." Then she said she was only kidding. Kids are cruel and the teasing I endured has stayed with me through the years.

As soon as I was old enough, 16, mom took me for a nose job. I did it over Christmas vacation and showed up on the bus in January with a new nose. Wow, that was a lot for a teenager. It was not well received. I looked better but I needed a revision.

At 17, I went for my second surgery. This time it was better, but I began to become obsessed with it. I told the doctor I was unhappy with the tip. He told me I was a spoiled kid. My mom loved the change and had hers done soon after. Hers was subtle and transformative. She looked gorgeous in the later years of her life. She looked the most beautiful later in life as Capricorns usually do.

The complications of my surgeries, however, made me feel broken and I became fearful of the camera. My mother's brother, my Uncle Jack, who also had nose surgery would say, "I took pictures of you and I had to throw them away." He had his surgery in the 1960s and it was also not well received. He was just giving me back what he had gotten, but it really damaged my self esteem. I was 19, and in college when I started getting cute again. A teacher at my college saw this and connected some dots for me.

At 20, I had an agent and was making money modeling. My pictures were not the best, but I was doing fashion shows and live appearances. When Donna Eastman, my agent, sent me on go-sees, I always got the job. She even paid for my portfolio.

When I was 21, I decided I hated the tip of my nose. I was at Montclair University and I ran into a girl from high school. She looked great. She had just had her nose done

The Lonely Boy

and was trying to became an actress. I got the name of her surgeon and went in for surgery a third time. This guy did a great job on the tip of my nose and made it look perfect. As I was healing though, I developed a blood clot and when he punctured it, it left me with a slight divot on one side.

I will say that people always found me attractive. I had attractive parents, but all these surgeries were not good for my mental health. I began to get a complex that I was disfigured. For years afterwards, I would go from surgeon to surgeon and they would all tell me the same thing: that I was a great looking guy. They said they wouldn't take my money, and told me I looked fine.

But the damage was done and I was scarred, not on the outside, but on the inside. I have to say I no longer believe in plastic surgery. There are always complications. Unless something is really wrong, don't mess with it. The surgeon told me himself, there is nothing better than natural and I agree. As I have matured, people have always weighed-in on my looks. When you are a guy, people think you are immune and will tell you the worst things about yourself. Mom once said to me, "How could a guy so good looking take such bad pictures?" She was right. That is something I never got right in my own life and am still working on today.

Many years later after a family funeral, my mom's cousin, who was in his 80s, was speaking at his son's repast. He was becoming a little senile and had no filters.

The Lonely Boy

Another person noticed me and asked him who I was. At 6'2" with blonde hair, blue eyes and a button nose, I didn't look like a typical paesan. He said, "That's Rich. Rich is really nice, but boy is he ugly!" I was crushed sitting there in my black cashmere v-neck sweater, Burberry shirt and tailored trousers. I had to sit through the next three hours feeling miserable about myself. I know I have not pursued some of my dreams because of trauma from my early years and particularly from my family. If I do anything with the rest of my life, I want to inspire young people to love themselves. I am still working on it.

I had many opportunities in my late teens and early 20s. I didn't pursue them though because I had a poor and unrealistic self image. I missed out on so many things that I really wanted to try. I wanted to be an actor and I came close to doing that. I wanted to live in New York City and explore all the opportunities the city had to offer.

I was an extra on an episode of a New York-based television show once. I was with hundreds of other people and several of my friends that day. I was picked out of the crowd of hundreds of people to sit next to the actor Telly Savalas in the season-opening show. I was with him for eight hours. Telly got shot in this scene and the camera was on me, the young blonde boy next to him. I obviously caught someone's eye. When we went to craft services for dinner they called for me to shoot it again. They didn't know my name so they kept asking for "the young blonde man in the white jacket." I became very scared and left. This was a great opportunity for me and it could have been a first credit for me to get my Screen Actors Guild (SAG) card. I blew it because I was afraid I was not attractive enough.

When I watched the episode air on television, you only saw the back of my head. That day was a gift and I didn't love myself enough to receive it and pursue my dreams. Any time there was media involved, I was always picked out of the crowd, especially when I was in L.A. Wonderful things presented themselves to me and I now realize I wasted those early gifts. Many of these opportunities never came to fruition because I had a bad self image. I hope that one day I will be able to make peace with myself and learn to love myself fully.

The Lonely Boy

Chapter 3   The First Big Crisis

As the seasons changed and time went on, I transitioned to middle school and my pre-teen years. My middle school was even more old-world and backward than my grammar school. It was small and very Italian Catholic. It was during that summer that I began to mature sexually. Of course, in the beginning I didn't know what was happening. I had lots of questions, but no resources to go to. Also, because I was more of a loner I was not interacting with other boys my age. At one point when my mother was driving us home from our swim club, she mentioned in passing that my body was changing. Several weeks later I overheard her asking my father to talk to me about my sexual maturity. He was not comfortable with this and brushed it off. Many years later I would find out that he was the victim of a childhood predator and had big issues with his own feelings and being able to communicate.

It was during this time that I began to notice that I was attracted to other males. I looked at both men and women. I was also attracted to women, but with men the attraction was a lot stronger. This really scared me and was something I did not want to happen. I did not want to hurt or embarrass my parents. This was a time when there was no outlet for a young boy in the suburbs to share his feelings. It became obvious that I was becoming troubled over something. I began to sink into my first bout of

The Lonely Boy

depression. When my 7th grade teacher brought my depression to my mother's attention, she realized she couldn't wait for my father to step in. It wasn't because he didn't care. He just didn't have the skills to help me.

My sweet, yet somewhat naive mother sought the help of the local parish priest. I had been an altar boy since I was 8 years old and this particular priest always had me work with him during his masses. He also officiated when my sister Jennifer was baptized. This same priest accidentally gave my sister Mary Anne First Holy Communion before she was ready because she was at one of my early morning masses before school started. I think because of these interactions, my mother felt comfortable with this man and felt he could help me.

On a particularly uneventful Tuesday night, the doorbell rang and it was Father. I watched my mother making coffee and talking with us in the kitchen. Father felt that I could not speak freely and he wanted to speak to me alone. My dad had recently finished our basement, so mom let us to go downstairs to have our talk. I was not prepared for this and was quite uncomfortable. He was very aggressive and got right into it. He asked me about becoming sexually aware and asked if I was masturbating. I think I told him no, but that wasn't not true. Not much else happened during that first visit, but Father insisted that we meet every week to try to get to the source of my depression.

The Lonely Boy

The next time we met and for the duration, we would meet on Saturday afternoons. This time he brought a book with him on sexuality. He began to show me pictures, first of naked women and then pictures of naked men. I was horrified. This was not something I wanted to do. He told me I would have homework and he wanted me to be able to talk freely using the names of body parts and not look away. Now I was quite scared. I felt that something was really wrong and when he left, I told my mother I didn't want him to return. She refused. He had assured her that we would make progress and she really wanted me to grow and start connecting with the other boys in the neighborhood.

The next week, Father showed up with two other men. We went down the basement and he brought out the book. He started pointing to male and female genitalia and wanted me to say the names out loud. I couldn't. I was too afraid. He persisted and I was able to repeat the names of the female organs. They were so foreign-sounding to me, they didn't seem as threatening. Then he pointed to the naked man and asked me to say the names of his body parts. I couldn't. He got forceful with me and got close to my body. Before I knew it he was taking my pants off. When I resisted he had the other men hold me down as he stripped me naked. I was a 13 year old boy!!! He told me he was going to spank me. That's when I realized the guy was a predator. He held me naked with the other men watching and spanked me. I could see he wanted me and

The Lonely Boy

enjoyed holding a young boy's body. I was terrified. I know to this day that I have trust issues and issues with my sexuality because of the trauma he caused me. I have blocked some of this out, but I don't recall any penetration, only fondling. After it was over I told my mother that I would not do this again. She refused, never dreaming of what was really happening.

One night that week I tried to tell her what he had done to me and she said she didn't want to hear it. She had no idea she brought a sexual predator into her house to molest her 13 year old son. Father would come every week and I only seemed to get worse. He always had a man with him and they would touch me and he would want me to touch them. This went on for months. I think it got to the point that he had to find a reason to stay. He decided he wanted me to start running track. He brought over two young college guys and I started running with them. He always wanted me to connect with men and to touch them sexually. He always had them take their pants down and wanted me to tell him how I liked looking at it. There was never penetration or oral sex that I can remember, but I was being sexually abused. Then out of the blue, on Holy Saturday, he came for another session. He told my mom that I was healed and that he would not return. I believe that in the beginning he thought I would start having sex with him but when time passed and I was so uncooperative, he gave up. I was the perfect target for a predator: a sweet cute blonde

The Lonely Boy

boy who was isolated and needy. I think he became attracted to me first when I was 8 years old. He always wanted me at his masses. I remember him hugging me hard and long and making me drink the leftover consecrated wine. I even remember walking to school after mass feeling a little buzzed. One time I got physically sick. The school nurse had to call my mother to pick me up. I think she told her I had a stomach bug. I'm also pretty sure he was sexual with those Rutgers boys and all the men he brought to the house to "heal" me. On our last session he told me that he knew I was attracted to men. He said that I should write down my feelings when I found myself feeling attracted. He also told me to get a journal and put my journal in a locked drawer and not let anyone see it. I did just that and I have been keeping a journal of my life experiences ever since.

I admitted to myself in writing that I was gay and wanted to be with another man. It was the worst thing I could do. My mother had no barriers. She unlocked my drawer, read my diary and confronted me with the news when I came home from school. It was heartbreaking what happened and how she made me feel. It would never be the same after this moment. She told me she was disgusted with me and told me not to tell my father. Her whole personality changed and she became as cold as ice.

The Lonely Boy

The next Christmas there were gifts for both of my sisters under the tree. I just got a card. In the card was a check. I got the message that I didn't matter to her any more.

I don't know how I got through that time in my life. No connections at school, no friendships of significance, and no love at home. No kid should ever have to live that way. I am not angry at my mother for what happened. In her mind, she felt tough love would straighten me out, but what I needed most of all was love and acceptance. I wasn't even with anyone yet. That wouldn't happen until I was 21. I was just a young lost kid who needed guidance and love. I guess that's why I never wanted children.

My years on Clifton Avenue were horrible for me. I was trapped and lost. I was not feminine or gay acting at all so I graduated 8th grade pretty much under the radar. I made it through, but with no connection to other kids, I always felt sad and alone.

One day that summer a song came on the radio on the way to our swim club. It was called "Lonely Boy" by Andrew Gold. I felt he was telling my story. It was about a boy who grew up feeling very unloved and unwanted. In the song it says, "My sister grew up, she married a man, he gave her a son, a warm and loving son. They dressed him warmly and they sent him to school. They taught him how to fight to be fight to be nobody's fool." I just knew that song was my story and that if my sister's firstborn child

The Lonely Boy

was a son, it would be true and the boy would have a special place in my heart.

By the end of that summer my mother decided I needed to toughen up. Instead of going to the co-ed Catholic high school in our town, she was sending me to the all boy's prep school a few towns over. The vibe was very different and I think she thought that a tougher all-male environment might change me.

I am someone who doesn't handle change very well. The new school was like a college campus. It was very different. I didn't know anyone there. The school's main focus was on Catholic education and sports. I never had so much phys. ed. in my life. I actually became good at track and soccer. In fact I got an A in gym. My mom was shocked!!!

I was very unhappy in this school. I was always alone and felt lost. Also, sexual things were happening between the boys. I once saw a guy giving oral sex under the stairwell right outside the Art classroom door. Older boys were touching me in the hallways as well. I hated it there and fell back into a second round of depression. I got great grades and I did better in sports than I ever had, but I was miserable.

I begged my mom to move me to the co-ed high school in town. She sent me to therapy instead. The therapist told her to let me change schools, so she finally did.

The Lonely Boy

I started the next year at the Catholic high school in my own town. It was close to home and I knew all the kids there, even though none were really friends. I began a friendship with a girl I knew from grammar school. We met on a school trip to the Statue of Liberty years earlier. I remember even on that very day I could tell she liked me and wanted to be friends with me. When she found out I was transferring to her school, she reached out to me right away and I became part of her clique. I was happy about this. I was part of something now, even though I would classify us as the nerd table. I was finally connecting with other kids. I came home, however, to a mother who had turned her attentions to my middle sister Mary Anne and had become obsessed with my sister's life. She couldn't give me the time of day.

So I became friendly with my friend's parents and was over their house a lot. Until of course, trouble began. The girl who befriended me decided she wanted to go out with me. She was a big girl and she was tough. I assumed she was gay too and we were good cover for each other to make it through Catholic high school in the 1980s. Now I was in trouble, as the group started pairing off into couples. I was coupled with someone I did not want to be with. She was quite aggressive and always wanted to kiss and fool around. I had to get out of it.

The summer after my sophomore year we were all at the 4th of July fireworks show. My parents were there too, but

The Lonely Boy

not with me. My mother ran into us and said she had to take my sister Jennifer to the rest room. She was obsessed with cleanliness and wanted to make sure my sister didn't sit down on a public toilet. My friend said she would hold my mom's purse while she took my youngest sister to the rest room. Well, we were in a big crowd and we got separated. At some point my friend lost my mom's purse. It was a terrible scene and my mother was screaming at me and at her. It was really awful. When I got home that night my mother wasn't talking to me. Several days passed with no communication. But, then I had an inspiration: Margaret was a big girl and I feared she would think I walked away from her because of her size. I didn't want to hurt her and would never tell her my true feelings. So I told her instead that my mother wouldn't let me see her anymore.

I assumed it would be the perfect solution. It wasn't at all. She wasn't sad. She was pissed, and she was determined to hurt me in any way she possibly could. We didn't talk for the rest of the summer and when I returned for my junior year, she proceeded to make my life hell. She and Frank, another guy in my circle, started a rumor that I had been raped in my previous all boy's school and that is why I transferred. The rumor spread quite quickly and I found myself alone in the cafeteria. This went on for a long time. When Valentine's Day came, I opened my locker. It was filled with garbage and a big sign that said HAPPY VALENTINE'S DAY FAG. Everyone saw it and I was

The Lonely Boy

called into the principal's office. The principal told Margaret and Frank that if I committed suicide it would be their fault. When would my torture ever end? No love at home, no friendships, no connections.

After that I just stopped paying attention in school. I just didn't care anymore. I purposely did not study or pay attention in my chemistry class because I think I was looking for my mom to notice me. Even though I was quite bright, I failed chemistry and had to go to summer school. There were six of us that failed chemistry and we were all called publicly into the principal's office on the last day of school. One of the other people who failed was Frank. Frank was in Margaret's social group, and I knew he was gay too. In fact I believed he was the one behind my Valentine's Day massacre to create a smoke screen for himself. I didn't trust him, but we were the only two boys in the summer school class and we were together every day.

He was very guarded and he could tell I knew about him. He told me one day in a coded way to protect myself. I got the message, although he did nothing to help me. Unlike me, he had sexual experience with men. In our junior year, we went to Spain where he was originally from. He snuck out and hooked up with someone in a gay bar. He dated a girl in our class and was with her on the trip, but I knew he was using her.

The Lonely Boy

My mother met Frank once. It was on my 16th birthday
and Frank had given me Erma Bombeck's classic
paperback, "If Life is a Bowl of Cherries, What am I Doing
in the Pits?" as a gift. It was an obvious put down. She told
me, "Don't trust this guy, he is jealous of you." The one
thing about my mother, she knew things and she was right.

On the first day of summer school, a beautiful young
woman introduced herself as our teacher. She was in her
mid-20s and quite pretty. I noticed from the first day of
summer school that she would stare at me. Not like I was
odd, but like she was interested in me. I brushed it off, but I
noticed it more and more as time went on.

My mother's anger towards me never went away. One
day when she was mad about something, she ripped my tee
shirt off my body and screamed, "Be normal!!!" It was
overwhelming for me. When her family came over one
Sunday, she told them, "Richard is in summer school with a
teacher that gave Mary Anne an A in that class." What a
shitty thing to do to a kid. I must admit, however, I enjoyed
the attention from my teacher. I started having my lunches
with her. She told me her parents owned a restaurant
nearby and that we should go there together some time.

On the last day of class, after I received my A, she took
me to lunch. We had a wonderful time and as she drove me
back to the school we stopped and parked. She told me I
reminded her of her high school boyfriend and then we

kissed. I couldn't believe it. Someone was interested in me!!!!!! It was really nice and I was attracted to her too.

I didn't see her again until senior year started. When I went up to her, she was a cold as ice. I guess she realized what she did and she got scared. The fickle finger of fate hit me and I was rejected yet again. My senior year was lonely and uneventful. My dad bought me an old used station wagon so I could take myself and my sister to school. They didn't even take me with them to pick out a car. I wondered if my mom was tired of driving me places and it was a way of getting away from me. I did love the freedom a car gave me and I started to become very independent.

Once a month my high school had something called "Flower Day." If you had a crush on someone, you could buy them a carnation through the school. The Catholic schools were always looking for money. Of course, after the rumors about me surfaced, no one really had much to do with me. I was sure that I'd never get a flower.

So I was shocked to find a flower on my desk in homeroom in the spring of my senior year. It turned out that friend of my sister's liked me. She was very pretty and wasn't enrolled in the school when the rumor came out. I hadn't gone to my Junior Prom but I decided to ask her to my Senior Prom. She said yes!!!! I had never had sex with anyone and I became confused about my sexuality after the encounter with my teacher. Maybe it was a phase I was

The Lonely Boy

going through. I was very happy about this. Maybe things would finally change for me.

I wanted to pick her up for the prom, but she changed her mind at the last minute and met me at our house. She looked beautiful, but she barely spoke. When we got to the prom, she was a dud. She wouldn't dance or participate. At first I was very accommodating to her, but then I got kind of mad. I spent a lot of money on the night and she wasn't even a good sport. Maybe she had heard the rumor and now I was poison to her too. I then did something I have never done before. Another girl asked me to dance and I left my date at the table and danced all night. This was my prom night and I was not going to have it end in another sad memory.

After the prom most kids went down to the Jersey shore for the weekend. I dropped off my date and went home alone. As I graduated from St. Peters High School a month later, I also left the church alone. No parties, no special plans with friends. I vowed that when I got to college in the fall things would be different.

The Lonely Boy

Chapter 4   I Began to Blossom

I was not given a choice about where I was going to college. My parents went to Middlesex County College and enrolled me without my knowledge. They said, "If you want to live with us, you will go to school there." They didn't care what I wanted at all. I wanted to go to the Fashion Institute of Technology in New York City to study interior design. They didn't even consider what I wanted. I was just so used to being unhappy I went along with it.

The funny thing was it was the beginning of a new and very happy phase in my life. I loved college. I was immediately popular and had a lot of friends right away. I even got on the Dean's List. I sprouted some newfound confidence and decided I was going to date girls. At one point I was dating two girls at the same time. This was a very happy time in my life. I rarely saw my family and was going to parties and working after school. It was great. It was like my past had been erased. I started to get serious with a girl named Paula. She was sweet and cute and a lot of fun. I brought her home to meet my family during the holidays. After my mom met Paula, I remember her saying, "When you were younger, I thought you might be gay." Her words weren't loving, but it was better than anger.

Paula had sexual experience. I was still a virgin and was very scared of sex, especially after the molestation I endured earlier in life. She didn't push me at first, but as time went on she started to push it. I remember taking her bra off and making out a lot.

One night we were at a holiday party and my old pal Frank reappeared. I was with my girlfriend Paula. He was alone and particularly friendly. He reached out to me and wanted to be friends. I never held grudges and I wanted to heal from our high school days.

After New Years he called and the two of us went out to dinner. He had moved to northern New Jersey with his family and was staying over that night at his sister's apartment in New Brunswick while she was away on winter break. He said he wanted to show it to me. I am someone who is very naive, especially back then. When we got there he pulled out a bottle of champagne that he had brought with him. He opened it and we drank it. As we were sitting there he opened up to me and told me he was gay. Then to my surprise he started touching me. He was interested in me. I was curious and touched back. I didn't like it though. We did not have good chemistry and I began to realize he was just looking for a hook up. He was not interested in being friends at all.

After that night I had terrible guilt. I told Paula what had happened and to my surprise, she said she wanted to continue dating. She said she didn't care because nothing really happened. More time passed and we continued to date but over time she began to fear I was cheating on her. It really killed the relationship. It eventually destroyed us and we broke up. That is what Frank was all about. If there was something good in my life he wanted to destroy it.

I have had a great deal of betrayal from friends. It was a pattern that would follow me throughout my life. Because of my family dynamics, I had a high tolerance for pain and it often clouded my judgment. I am someone who values friendship very highly. I love connecting with other people and will do anything for someone I consider a friend. Frank would come back into my life time after time like the prodigal son. I always took him back with no judgment. In the end, I always got burned.

I really loved my college days. There was always someone around and I began to blossom and develop confidence. There were a big group of us that hung out in the cafeteria in between classes. Sometimes there were 10 to 15 of us. We were all friends and I am still friends with many of them to this day. I was invited to parties every weekend and I was now never alone. One dull Monday morning a new girl sat next to me. She was a sweet bubbly girl dressed to the nines. Her name was Dawn. She was extremely warm and we connected right away. She and I started spending a great deal of time together. I went to pick her up one night and I got to meet her parents. I fell in love with her mom, Dee, the minute I met her. This lady was the opposite of my mother. She was fun and treated me with kindness and dignity. I miss her to this day.

The Lonely Boy

Dawn and I spent so much time together I didn't know if we were dating or not. One day we sat in my car in the school parking lot talking for hours.

Finally she said, "Rich, I know."

"What do you know?" I asked.

"I know you're gay," she replied.

I couldn't believe it. She knew and she still wanted to be a part of my life. Not in spite of it, but maybe because of it. I never met a woman who understood that before. I guess you could say, in a kind way, respectfully, she was my first "fag hag." The pretty bubbly girl who would rather hang with the gay guys that worshipped her than the jerky straight guys who gave her grief.

I loved our friendship. We did everything together and her mother accepted me and treated me like a son. I was so starved for love and attention at home it was exactly what I needed. Dawn also had whole group of gay friends. They accepted and embraced me too. We were like a 1980s Will and Grace and I loved it.

She went with me to my first gay bar, but I never wanted anyone there. I was much happier being with her. I loved being part of a family and I now had a place to be. This was a very happy time for me. I began to socialize with several of her male friends and we started to go to bars, first with her, but eventually without her. I noticed over time she started to lose interest. I was devastated. I had faced such rejection in life I didn't want to lose my new second family.

The Lonely Boy

I would hold onto them for as long as I could, but it was never the same after I starting dating men. That's the problem with the straight girl/gay guy relationship. It has a shelf life.

I decided after that I wanted to try to date a guy to see if it was even really something I wanted. I started dating men for the first time at 19. No one special, I just put myself out there. I used to go to a small local bar called The Den. It was in a really bad area, but it was beautiful inside. It was in an old town house with exposed brick walls, a baby grand piano and a courtyard. One of the things that happen when you put yourself in a gay bar, especially in a small town, is that you become aware that you are not alone. I saw several people there on Monday nights that I never thought were gay. One of them was an old friend of my dad's from the Navy who was married. The other was a former neighbor who also was married. The worst one was Jeff.

I had a friend named Lucy who was 20, a year older than me. She was a nice girl who was very pretty and she'd recently gotten engaged. Lucy and her fiancé stopped by my parent's house one night and my mom opened up a bottle of champagne for us to toast Lucy and Jeff.

The next day mom said, "I'm worried about Lucy. All this happened too fast and something just doesn't seem right about it."

The Lonely Boy

"Jeff seems very nice," she continued, "but I just get a bad feeling."

Mom just knew things about people. She had a certain sense and she was usually right.

One night, I was in The Den and I saw Jeff there with another man. He saw me and quickly left. When I got home, I didn't know what to do. I thought about it all night. I decided to tell mom I was with friends at a restaurant two doors down and we saw Jeff coming out of the gay bar. I talked and she just listened. I never heard anything about it again.

I found out many years later that my mom told Lucy Jeff may be gay. I feel terrible about it now. Mom didn't want Lucy to get hurt. I understand that, but I wish I wasn't the messenger.

The bar began to fill the void that Dawn left as she backed away. One night I was very blue because I missed Dawn. I told my mother about it. She said, "I don't blame her. I wouldn't go on with a guy if there was no future." I was just wasting my time with mom.

That night I dragged myself to the gay bar, I was so down. I was 19 years old and a real blonde twink. Due to my depression and poor self esteem, I had no idea what I offered at that time. An older man came over to me and bought me a drink. His name was Walter. He was from Ohio and had moved to New Jersey for an engineering job. He was smart and confident and a real man. He told me he couldn't believe someone as handsome as me would even talk to him.

"He thinks I'm handsome?" I thought. I have always had problems with my self esteem. Even to this day, I hate to have my picture taken because I don't feel attractive. This was new territory for me. I had been praying for a nice man to come into my life and he was definitely it. I mentioned to him that I wondered what he would look like without a moustache and he came to the door on our first date clean shaven. I told him I wish he lived closer and he moved to my town to be closer to me. He knew I was a virgin and he didn't push me to have sex. Walter and I had chemistry. He really turned me on and was a great kisser. I felt safe with him and I trusted him.

I was turning 20 and he invited me over for my birthday. At the end of the evening he handed me an envelope. In it was a plane ticket to New Orleans. I couldn't believe it. No one had ever been this kind to me before. I had graduated from community college was in Montclair University now. I lived on campus and didn't come home on weekends because I felt rejected by my mother. My parents would never know if I went away with an older man.

I got on a plane by myself and flew to New Orleans. The flight had a layover, I forget where. While I was waiting, a very handsome man started talking to me. He got on the plane with me and because the plane was empty, he sat

The Lonely Boy

down right next to me. I remember he shared his corn and crab chowder with me and we talked nonstop.

He was from New Orleans and wanted to spend time with me when we got there. He said he wanted to take me out on his boat. He was hitting on me big time. I wasn't sure at first because he had a wedding ring on, but as more time passed I realized it. I told him I was meeting my friend Walter at the airport and I guess he assumed he was another kid like me. He stayed with me when we were getting our luggage. When he saw that Walter was a 6'4" grown man, he left and we never spoke again.

I felt very special for the first time in my life. Maybe I was special after all and I was worthy of true love and kindness. Walter knew I was a virgin and got double beds as I demanded. Now, I wish I had slept with him.

Walter had to work during the day, so I explored the city by myself. I went to the New Orleans Jazz Festival alone. Gloria Estefan picked me out of a crowd of thousands to come up onstage with her and throw a beach ball out into the crowd. What was going on? I was not special. I was not worthy of such kindness. It was hard for me to process positive attention after all the sad and lonely years.

That trip was a great gift. Walter and I went to the best restaurants. We were both big eaters and we ate our way through the city. I was young and had no experience with drinking. I drank every night. One night I left my shoes at the front entrance of the Weston Hotel and walked through

The Lonely Boy

the lobby barefoot at 3 am. The following morning the bellman handed me my shoes. I gave up a perfectly good pair of new shoes because I was too embarrassed to admit they were mine.

The next week was Easter. I went home for the holiday and my mom asked me why I was so tan? I said I went to a tanning salon. She never asked any other questions. She barely took an interest in my life. She would call me at college from time to time, but always to check up on my sister.

One night I brought Mary Anne some food and when I opened the door I saw she was smoking pot. I could have told my mother, who now devoted all her energy to Mary Anne, but that would have broken mom's heart. I kept it to myself. Even with the bad treatment I still loved her and longed to return to a time when we were connected. I think mom must have known that I was dating but she just couldn't deal with it. The anger was gone now but we were just not in each other's life anymore. I still loved her very much though and would have done anything to be in her life. When I used to hear the song "Think of Me" by Todd Rundgren, I would think of her and our estrangement. It is a sadness I will never heal from.

Walter and I continued to date. I was doing well in school and had many friends. I was also taking an acting class as an elective and my teacher felt I was talented. When I did

The Lonely Boy

my final scene with my partner Patty, I was voted best in
our class.

My teacher passed my name around and I started to get
some small acting jobs. I started making industrial films for
the EPA. I did a little modeling. I even had an agent. I was
in a low budget local cable soap opera called "Young at
Heart" and even an extra in an episode of a national
television show. One day the actor Peter Bergman from
"The Young and the Restless" came to our school. He
pointed to me and said, "You are going to be an actor. You
stand out and you will be successful." I will never forget
that moment.

I really started to feel good about myself. Walter wanted
to have sex with me and was putting pressure on me to
move forward. I decided I was not ready and I broke up
with him. He was probably the man I should have spent my
life with, but I just met him too soon. I was just too young
to settle down and very scarred from the molestation in my
early years. Some days though, I still regret this decision.
He was and is a very good man.

I was single again but very happy. I then had a little blip
in my life. A random eye test had revealed I had no
peripheral vision. The doctor asked me to tell him how
many fingers he was holding up and I said, "What fingers?"
The test revealed I needed to do something and fast. They
sent me to a specialist at the Wills Penn Eye Hospital in
Philadelphia.

The Lonely Boy

My dad took me to every appointment and supported me through my surgery. My mom was not involved at all. On the night after I came home from the hospital, I had a dream or a vision that woke me up. It was about 1:00 am and I was sweating from the anesthesia. The dream or vision included my nana. She told me that she was in heaven and that it was a great place. I said, "I should tell dad." Nana replied, "Your dad already knows. Tell your mother."

I got up and went downstairs and told mom. She and Mary Anne were both still up talking and when I told them, mom reacted in a way I did not see coming. She said, "Oh my God, I'm going to die." It really upset her. As soon as I saw her reaction, I regretted telling her. It was probably just the anesthesia withdrawal, so I never mentioned it again.

After a few weeks I was back to school and work. I wore special sunglasses for a few weeks but that was it. It would be the first in a series of health problems that would affect me throughout my life.

My life moved forward and my agent had me working for a marketing firm in Long Island now. They had me in a tuxedo giving out samples of Aramis cologne all over the tri-state area. I was also showing model homes dressed preppy in Ralph Lauren Polo for a local builder in Princeton. At 20 my life had been transformed. I was so happy and confident. I wasn't afraid of anything and I looked forward to all the opportunities I had ahead of me.

The Lonely Boy

One night I went out to The Den with my friend Rob. He introduced me to a guy who was his cousin. His name was Brian. The guy was gorgeous. He was 6'4" with black hair, blue eyes, and a cleft in his chin. I was immediately attracted and so was he. At 20 I looked more like 16 and this guy loved twinks.

Brian asked me out that night and we planned to meet at his house. On the day before the date I got a call from Rob. Rob told me not to go out with Brian. He said Brian was not a good guy. He then admitted he was interested in his own cousin and asked me not to go. I called Brian and tried to cancel. I wound up telling him the truth and we went out. It was Memorial Day weekend 1986. When I drove up his street I couldn't believe how beautiful it was. The tree-lined street had grand old houses from the 1930s. It was and still is beautiful today. He lived in the guest house of his boss's estate home. I pulled down the long driveway and when I went in it was very charming.

He drove me in his dark sports car to a local Mexican restaurant and we had a great date. We went back to his house and he made us little individual strawberry shortcakes for dessert. It was the best date I had ever been on. I was crazy about this guy. He had this indescribable something that I have never felt with anyone before or since. To this day, if he is in my proximity, I can feel him before I see him.

The Lonely Boy

We talked for hours and I mentioned in passing that I was a romantic and I hoped one day I'd have a special someone to share Valentine's Day with. On our next date, I went to his place for dinner. When I opened the door, he had the entire place decorated as if it was Valentine's Day. Brian showed me his calendar, which he amended for the occasion, and it *was* Valentine's Day, in June. No detail was overlooked. I was in love with this guy. I spent the night with him. It was the best night of my life. When I woke up in the morning in his arms, I was in heaven. We had sex again. I was not afraid at all, I was ready. Our summer together was magical. One weekend we stayed in bed from Friday night until Monday morning. I thought maybe my years of agony were finally over and life had balanced itself. It is now 2017 and I look back at 1986 as the happiest year of my life. It seems so far away now some 30 years later. I sometimes wonder if that was the greatest peace and happiness I will ever know.

I was 21 now and I was confident, successful, and loved by the perfect guy. I stayed with him on a beautiful estate in the guest cottage. He was gorgeous and I loved to look at him. I loved the way he looked and smelled. He was everything to me. My relationship with Brian had also boosted my confidence. On day when mom was giving me grief, I looked at her and finally just said, "When you get old I am going to put you in a nursing home." It was the single worst thing I could think of saying. And then,

The Lonely Boy

because she was such a germaphobe, I added, "A dirty one."

But instead of being angry with me, we both just burst out laughing. She knew I had had enough and I think she could see I was really starting to find my own way.

The marketing company I was working for at the time was looking for a woman in her 40s to demo a new exercise bike. She had to be in great shape and wear a form fitting running suit. I recommended her for it and she got the job. So at one point I became her boss!!! Life throws us strange curves.

September came and I had to go back to school. During my senior year in college, I decided to rent a third floor suite in an old Victorian house. I set up my schedule so I had three days with Brian and four days at school. He gave me a key and I drove down every Wednesday to have dinner with him to break up the week. On my ride down I would cut through Route 22 and pass Uncle Joe's exit. I always hoped one day that my cousins would be back in my life, but I was way too shy to ever stop.

Our weekends were spent having sex and we barely left that romantic cottage. I was the happiest I had ever been in my life. It was the only time I had true mental peace. I introduced him to all my friends but I began to get the feeling they didn't like him. I couldn't understand why. I guess I was clueless and in love. They used to refer to him as "the seahorse" because he had a long head and a cleft

The Lonely Boy

chin. I alone did not see this guy's obvious shortcomings. The relationship would not last.

My first cause for concern came in November when with almost no notice he went down to Florida without me to buy a classic car. It was a 1965 Lincoln Continental with suicide doors. This guy was so interesting and he had great style. I was learning a lot from him, but when he didn't take me with him, I was worried and hurt. The night he came home, he drove directly to my apartment in Montclair and left a bag of oranges in my car with a sweet note.

When Thanksgiving came, we both spent the day with our families, but rushed back to be together at night. When Christmas Eve came, he bought me a beautiful black leather travel bag. He said it was for my things when I came back and forth from school, but I began to wonder if he was sending me a subtle message that I should be packing to go. I had keys to his house and a whole dresser there full of my things but I began to feel pangs of insecurity.

He went to Florida again for New Years and once again he went alone. Now I knew something was wrong. Had he met someone in Florida? I was still very much in love with him, and I was becoming vulnerable. I was so afraid I was losing him, I began to become insecure and it only made things worse. He would do sweet things for me all the time like make me breakfast and start my car in the winter so it

The Lonely Boy

was warm when I left for school. But I could tell that something was changing.

In February of 1987, I stopped home to see my parents. It was a Thursday night and my mother and father were holding hands. That was a first. In fact, my mother lost circulation in her hands and they were trying to get it back. My mother was not feeling well and went for some tests at the hospital the next day. I had dinner with them that night. I remember it was a Friday during Lent so we had linguini with white clam sauce. My mom had become an excellent cook and it was really good. At the end of the meal, the phone rang. It was her doctor. He told her to pack a bag and get to the hospital. Then the phone rang again. It was the hospital lab. They told her to get to the hospital right away.

It was my mom's worst nightmare. Just as she had always feared, she was sick. I remember her knowing this was it. As she left the house she hugged each one of her children, including me, long and hard. I think she knew she would never come home again.

My parents didn't tell us anything at first, but when I was back in school on Monday my mom told me on the phone that she had leukemia. She told me she was not going to tell the girls yet, but she wanted me to know. She also confided her fears in me. She told me, "Your own mortality is the hardest thing you will ever have to face." I was devastated.

I called my mother's brother, my Uncle Jack, and we sobbed on the phone together from my college apartment. I

The Lonely Boy

drove down to be with Brian but he wasn't very compassionate. In fact, I acutely felt him pull away in the weeks that followed. Brian was spending less and less time with me so when his birthday came around in early March, I decided to do something special for him. I baked him a birthday cake. I had never baked anything before in my life and I frosted it too early so it looked terrible. I brought it to him and bought him a very expensive red Ralph Lauren shirt that he once admired. I couldn't afford it, so I had to open up my first credit card to pay for it. I wanted him to know how much he meant to me. We had cake together, but I went back to my parents' house that night. I decided to move back home to be close to my mom and to spend time with my youngest sister, who was only 13 at the time. I wanted to comfort her.

In a way, I was prepared for this because my mom told me many times she would die young and of cancer. She laid out her instructions early on and I tried to honor all of them. On Monday morning March 16th, I got ready for school. It was over an hour away and I still had that unreliable old station wagon. An inner voice told me not to go to school, but to go to the hospital instead. It was 8 am and I went to the hospital and stayed with my mother all day.

At about 1:00 in the afternoon her best friend Joanne came in. I was very afraid to touch my mother who was now on a ventilator. Joanne made me hold her hand and I

The Lonely Boy

did that for hours. I spent hours telling her I loved her and that I wanted her to get better. At 5 pm my dad came in and figured out I never went to school. I asked him if he was mad and he said he wasn't. He said it was enough for one day and told me to go home. I told my mom one last time that I loved her and then I left.

That night I grabbed something to eat alone and called my mom's friend Joanne hoping to talk, but no one answered. Shortly after I left, my mother had a brain hemorrhage and she was now brain dead. Dad didn't tell me anything when he came home later that night. The next day was March 17th, St. Patrick's Day, and my father made sure I went to school. I had a big final presentation and graduation was only six weeks away.

The next night was March 18th. Late that night the phone rang. Dad went alone to the hospital and came back very quickly. I knew when he returned so quickly that she was gone. She was only 47 years old.

Dad called my sister Mary Anne but she didn't return his calls. She didn't even come home that night. I called Brian and told him I needed him now more than ever. He told me flat out that that he didn't know if he could be there for me. He didn't call again or come to the wake or funeral. I was devastated. My mom was gone and now he was gone. I couldn't tell anyone and it became too much for me. On the night of the wake, I passed out on the floor of the funeral home.

The Lonely Boy

The services went according to mom's instructions. We had closed casket and we buried her in a mausoleum. We decided to have the repast at the house to be close to home. When everyone filed in, Mary Anne, Jen and I went up to Mary Anne's bedroom and sat on her bed for a long while talking. The thought of going downstairs to a kitchen without my mother was something we had to build up our courage to do. We eventually went down and mingled with the mourners.

I stayed close to home in the weeks that followed and I learned to cook so Jennifer could have some continuity in her life. Mary Anne went right back to college. Shortly before my mother got sick we watched a movie on television together. The plot involved a young girl who decided she would do the right thing for someone else even though it would get her into trouble. My mother turned to me and said, "I would like to think Mary Anne would be the kind of person to put someone else first, but I just don't know." It was the only time she ever acknowledged that Mary Anne was an uncompassionate person. It was the first predictor of something that would blow up into a life altering event many years later. Like I said, mom just knew things.

A few days after the funeral, I got a phone call from Brian. He was stuck on the road and he needed me to come rescue him. My dad was listening to my conversation. About a month before my mom got sick, my father

The Lonely Boy

overheard a telephone conversation between Brian and me and figured out we were together. He accepted it and it was never discussed again. When he heard that Brian was looking for my help now but was not there for me when I buried my mother, he forbid me to go. He said, "This guy is a loser." He was totally right, but I went anyway. I picked up Brian and got his car to the service station. On the way back to his house I parked and we talked. I said, "DO YOU UNDERSTAND WHAT I HAVE JUST BEEN THROUGH?!" He answered in a very cold voice, "When it happens to my mother I'll deal with it." I saw the other side of this guy now. He could be incredibly cold and unloving. I dropped him off and went home.

Several days later he called and he picked me up. We took a drive down to the shore. When we were almost there I asked him to turn around. He did and I went home. We never slept together again. We barely even spoke.

Still grieving, one night I was out with a friend of mine and I asked him for advice. He told me that if I loved Brian I should fight for him. I took my friend's advice and did just that. I went out and bought the best pair of jeans I could buy and a great shirt with that new credit card. I got my hair cut and it really looked good. I stopped at the bakery and bought his favorite apple pie. We often would share desserts together. That was his thing with me.

I rang his doorbell and told him I loved him and needed him. I begged him not to leave me. He never even let me in.

The Lonely Boy

He hugged me goodbye through the doorway and closed the door. I stood there with the pie box still in my hands. As I drove down his driveway, I thought to myself my life was a circle. I was at the bottom for most of my life and then things had finally started to get better. When I reached the top of the circle I was with the love of my life. Now I had a sharp fall back to the bottom where I was alone and lost again. A feeling I knew all too well, a lost and lonely boy.

The Lonely Boy

Chapter 5   A New Direction

A year passed by quickly and I was still living at my father's house with Jennifer. I wanted to remain close to home. Mary Anne stayed in the dorms at school. I graduated from college and got a job in sales for a large hotel chain. It was a time of much change. My dad began to realize how hard and lonely his life would be now and he became increasingly mean. I don't blame him. He was a widower way too soon and was left with thousands of dollars in unpaid medical bills.

He wasn't working much and he was having a hard time both emotionally and financially. He had been in the middle of a big construction job and was fired right after mom died. I went with him back to the jobsite because he had to get his things out of there quickly. I think he took his feelings out on me the most because I was there. He didn't want me to leave though. He was very unhappy my sister Mary Anne did not come home as well.

The house felt particularly lonely after Mom passed, and shortly afterwards a strange thing happened. My mom would never let us have a dog. She was a clean freak. No animals would ever have been allowed in the house, but a few weeks after her death a beautiful white Samoa appeared in our yard with no tags or collar. The dog had intense blue eyes and was gorgeous. It really helped us heal. I can't help but wonder if she sent it to us to help us in our grief.

One day as I was walking the dog, I ran into my friend Keith. Keith was a friend of Dawn's and he told me that he once lived in the garden apartment complex across the highway from where my dad lived. He said the apartments were rent controlled and I could get a studio very cheaply.

I was anxious to get away from my dad because he was becoming verbally abusive. I was still healing from a broken heart and the unresolved issues with my mother. One night when dad and I were talking about mom he said, "You know she didn't love you." I will never forget that. I was more angry than hurt. I know my mother loved me. She was very unhappy that I was gay, but I felt her love and knew it was there. Dad putting that on a 22-year-old was way too much. I knew I had to get out of there.

I remembered what Keith had told me about the apartments and in March of 1988 I signed a lease for an apartment of my own across the highway. It kept me close enough to keep an eye on Jen, while allowing me to protect myself from dad. I rented a large studio with a separate galley kitchen, a dressing room and a full bath. I loved it and it was the best thing for me.

I started decorating it right away. I put a wood floor in the kitchen along with a great backsplash. I put in wall-to-wall carpeting. I painted every room and put in new light fixtures. This is where my passion for interior design really

The Lonely Boy

began. I made the so place so beautiful people started telling me I should do it for a living. I never considered that I could make a good living at it back then. I was in hotel sales and was content with that at the time.

After the place was done, I started to realize that I was ready to start dating again. It had been a year since Brian and I had broken up and I was very lonely. He was the only man I ever loved and the only man I ever wanted to be with. One night at 2:30 am I received a phone call. It was from Jeff, Lucy's short-lived fiancé, the guy I outed to my mother. He was confronting me with outing him. He found out I had moved and he'd gotten my new number. He started saying sexual things to me and I hung up on him. This happened on and off for a few months. He always called in the middle of the night. One night I finally said, "Please stop calling. I recently lost my mom to cancer and I am suffering with grief and depression." When he heard that she had died he never called again. What a jerk.

It was 1988 and there was no Internet yet. If you were gay and wanted to meet someone, you had to go to a gay bar. There was only one gay bar in town and it was near Rutgers University. Monday night was the big night there. I decided to go out and was having an OK time until Brian walked in. He was extremely cold. He passed me quickly and told me how cute I looked. After a few quick words, he walked away and left shortly after with another young guy. It broke my heart. This was the guy I gave my virginity to.

The Lonely Boy

I had lost everything and he couldn't care less. He bought himself a new white Corvette and left with some other twink. I think I cried every night for the next three weeks. I was so heartsick I started to get physically sick. I stopped eating and sank into a serious depression. I started having stomach pains, losing hair, and losing weight. Every time I went to the bar, Brian was there. Sometimes he didn't acknowledge me at all. One night I decided to call him and another guy answered. When Brian picked up the phone, he told me he met someone else and not to call again. Another day I took a drive down to the shore and in the distance I saw Brian with someone else. I watched the two of them walking on the beach together in silhouette. The guy kind of looked like me and was around my age. What did this guy have that I didn't? I loved Brian so much I thought I would die without him. I felt my life would never be the same again and it never was.

Sometime later, in the middle of the night, I woke up in terrible pain. I went to the bathroom and there was blood in my stool. I knew something was very wrong. I called my dad and he took me to the hospital and they admitted me. I had developed ulcerative colitis.

It was at this time a friend of mine started to spend a great deal of time with me. His name was Rick. I had gotten to know him through Dawn. He brought me home from the hospital and stayed with me while I recovered. I knew he had feelings for me, but I was not over Brian yet. He was very good to me though and he filled a great void in my life. Rick and I did everything together as I slowly began to recover. Eventually I went into remission. My life was busy but I was still very sad inside.

One night I had planned to meet Rick for his birthday. When I was on my way home from work there was a traffic pile up. I decided to cut through some side streets and my car was broadsided by a Chevy Caprice sedan. I was hit so hard, my car flipped upside down. I was unconscious. When I came to, I was locked upside down in my seat. People were screaming on the street and two men with pocket knives climbed into the car and cut me out of the seat. They pulled me out by my feet and put me on the grass by the side of the road. I heard someone in the crowd say, "Oh no, Connie did it again."

By the time the ambulance arrived, the two men that had helped me were gone. The accident occurred only a few blocks from the hospital where my mom died a year earlier. Not knowing how badly I was injured, I asked the ambulance crew to take me to another hospital, Robert Wood Johnson, instead and they did. I didn't want my dad to have to return to St. Peter's Hospital so soon after my mom's death.

I had several broken ribs and spent the night in the hospital. Once again when I got home Rick took care of me. As time passed, Rick became my best friend. I loved

The Lonely Boy

him, but only as a friend. He wanted more, but I couldn't return those feelings.

By 1989, I was starting to date again and Rick was not happy about it. I always preferred older men because of their maturity level. I met a guy named Dennis who was 20 years my senior. He was sexy and mature, and unlike Brian, he introduced me to his friends and family right away. Once in a while though, Dennis would smoke pot and his personality would change dramatically. He went from being a very sweet man to being a nightmare. I have no tolerance for drugs of any kind so after a while we went our separate ways.

My youngest sister was turning 16 that year. When I turned 16 my parents had a small party for me, and they hosted one for Mary Anne when she turned 16 too. I decided to phone Mary Anne at work to ask if we could meet with my dad at his house to talk about it. She had graduated college and was now living with dad and working locally for a nearby health insurance company. She agreed and I got to the house at about 7 p.m. As I was coming up the driveway, she was pulling out of it to visit her boyfriend. She didn't even stop the car to say hello.

Mary Anne did not respect me or take anything I said seriously. I think she developed a cracked sense of entitlement after my mother's death. Now back at home, she was the woman of the house, but she lacked the warmth and nurturing instinct that usually came with the mother role. She had her own agenda and didn't care about anyone but herself. When I got inside dad was waiting for me. He put on tea as he always did and we got out mom's red address book. We then put a list of names together for the party. It was only two weeks away so I made phone calls from his house and we invited about 25 guests. We finished up sometime later and I went back to my apartment for the evening. About 11:45 pm the phone rang and woke me up. It was my dad. He was quite upset.

I asked what was wrong. He said Mary Anne came home and was furious that you planned a party without her. She said how dare you plan a party in her house without her there.

"Dad you know I called her first and she agreed to meet to talk about it," I said. "She chose to go out and not to meet with us."

"You have to un-invite everyone," he replied.

"Dad, you don't invite people to a party and then take it back," I said.

"Well," he said, "you can't have the party here."

I was so upset with him. I just said I had to get to bed. My dad really wanted a relationship with Mary Anne. He missed my mother terribly and they looked very much alike. The difference was that Mary Anne was as cold as ice. She was completely unlike mom in every way. Dad was just so happy to have her under his roof now; I think he would have done whatever he had to do to keep her there.

The Lonely Boy

My dad was a simple man and eventually starting dating again, but he never gave any of the women he met a chance. When they got the least bit close to him, he ended it. I think he felt Mary Anne was a wife figure in a way and when she rejected him, he sought out any way he could to get her attention. The next night dad and I discussed Jen's birthday and he was adamant that he would not hold the party at his home. My apartment was a studio, and it was way too small for 25 guests. I had no idea what to do.

The following day I talked to my boss about it and he gave me the name of another hotel in the area that would give me a good deal on a party as a favor to him. The hotel I worked at was very expensive and I would never be able to afford to hold the party there, even with my employee discount. I brought a friend from work with me and we booked the party. I even got my friend to be a DJ.

I invited Mary Anne and her boyfriend, of course, as well as all the original guests. Everyone showed except Mary Anne and Norman. They said they had another party and didn't even stop by. The party came at a rough time for me, since I had gone back to school at night to get my real estate license and the state test was the morning of the party. Without any help from my father and sister it was going to be tough, but I pulled it off. I took the state licensing test in the morning then picked up the cake in the afternoon and decorated the space. This was the first time my father really let me down and I was very disappointed in him. I never told him how I felt, because I knew he was still grieving the loss of my mom, but he really let me down.

In the end, the party was a success. Dad was out on the dance floor with his in-laws and friends, but he let me pick up the check for his daughter's Sweet 16 Party without flinching. The party cost more than I expected and I think I bounced my rent check that month.

I was beginning to realize just how much power Mary Anne had over my often weak father and that this was not a good thing for him or for me.

The Lonely Boy

Chapter 6   Celebrations and Rites of Passage

In 1990, I started a new job where I quickly became Director of Sales for a new hotel company. I also started a side career in real estate. I started making good money and managed to put some away. I decided I wanted to move further west and buy my first home. I was 25 now and was ready to stop grieving over Brian and my mom's death and make a new life for myself. I dated a lot and was popular.

It was about this time that my sister Mary Anne announced she was marring her boyfriend Norman. The guy she was marrying was a problem. No one in the family liked him. Mary Anne looked like my mom. She was beautiful. This guy was fat and homely and a real hothead. My father hated him and begged her not to marry him. At one point, dad even told his friends that they broke it off.

Norman was a homophobe and he hated me. He never gave me any respect. He actually tried to get the wreckage from my car accident towed to his cousin's shop so he could make money off me, but he never even bothered to see how I was. The guy was a dick. He was abrasive to everyone he came in contact with. Mary Anne was already as cold as ice and my dad feared he would lose her altogether if she married Norman. He was also worried that Norman would exclude me from the family and cause trouble for me.

The Lonely Boy

Mary Anne only cared about herself and went forward with the marriage. She went full steam ahead even though my dad told her outright that he just couldn't handle it. While she was working out the wedding logistics, at one point she mentioned in passing that she tried to get a hold of Father. This was the priest who accidentally gave her First Holy Communion and who molested me. She wanted him to perform the ceremony. She told me she was shocked to learn that he was now in a mental institution. I, on the other hand, was not surprised. I never shared my experiences with her but I was glad I wasn't going to see him again. I assumed he was hiding from his sins and all the boys whose lives he must have ruined along the way.

I was also really upset that Mary Anne couldn't grasp how hard it would be for dad to handle a wedding without my mother. It was so typical of her to just do what she wanted with no thought of the consequences to other people.

I had no feelings for Mary Anne by this time. She was empty and cold, but I had a soft spot for Jennifer. I really loved her and felt protective over her. When Jennifer was 10 months old, my mother slipped on the stairs and fell with her in her arms. For awhile, we didn't know if Jennifer was going to be all right. It scared me so much that I never forgot it. This made her very special to me from that moment on. The reason I moved home and stayed for a year after mom died was to be there for her.

The Lonely Boy

One day in the real estate office, I saw an announcement about a new townhome development in Bedminster, New Jersey. It was about 45 minutes northwest of New Brunswick and a really nice area known for its equestrian roots. I fell in love with the area and found a floor plan I liked. I put down a deposit and set up a date to take my dad to the jobsite, where they were just starting to frame the buildings.

As fate would have it, on the way up, we passed Brian on the road. I went limp when I saw him. Whenever I began to feel good about myself again, this guy would magically appear and bring me down. My dad asked what was wrong. I told him that Brian was in the car next to us. My dad went ballistic. He gave him the finger. He started screaming, "You asshole!" He actually put his foot over mine on the accelerator and tried to hit him with the car. I never ever saw dad lose control like that. I guess he saw how much this guy deeply hurt me. He also felt that Brian was responsible for my colitis and depression. Dad was also worried because at 25, I was 6'2" and weighed only 165 pounds. I was way too thin and had trouble eating. Whenever I get very thin it is because I am suffering from depression. There is mental illness on both sides of my family, but I feel like my depression is more from the Marino side.

In spite of the Brian sighting, we went to see the new place and my dad talked me into buying a bigger unit. He

The Lonely Boy

was right. He loved the new area but was unhappy that I was moving so much further away.

We were all growing up now and I think the further away I got from 21 Clifton Avenue, the less painful it was for me. The void my mother left was vast and time only made me miss her more and wish that things had worked out differently.

Mary Anne and Norman didn't have much to do with me. I never saw or heard from them. So it was quite a surprise one night when I got a late phone call in my apartment from Mary Anne. She and her fiancé liked the hotel I worked at and she asked if I could get them a deal for their wedding. I told her of course I would. I went overboard and also helped her with her honeymoon and the transportation.

I did not like Norman, but I felt my mom would want me to be there for my family, no matter what. So I did whatever I could. As the wedding got closer, Mary Anne picked her bridal party and asked Jennifer to be maid of honor. I, of course, was not included. One day my dad called me and told me he wanted to pay for Mary Anne's shower. Jennifer was far too immature to plan it and without a wife to guide him, dad thought it was his obligation to pay for it. He asked me if I would take care of the details since I was working in the hotel business and I knew how to plan and run a party. I found the perfect spot and booked the shower. On the day of the event, I dropped off dad's check and I am told by my Aunt Maria it went well.

It was becoming evident that Norman did not want me in his family. I was the only sibling who wasn't in the wedding party, and he made sure I was not invited to his bachelor party. One day I got a call from his best man asking why my father was refusing to come to the bachelor party. His best man knew I was not invited and went through me anyway to get to my dad. This was the beginning of a stormy relationship with Norman that would end in terrible tragedy many years later.

The wedding day arrived and as I left the church at the end of the mass, my mother's friend Joanne—the one who had helped me hold my mother's hand on the last day I spent with her—grabbed my arm and walked down the aisle with me.

"Richard," she said, "why aren't you in the wedding party?! This guy is an asshole. Your mother would not be happy with who your sister has chosen." I was touched that she was worried about me and what would happen to the family now that this guy was in the picture.

Time marched on and my condo was almost ready. I had already given notice on my apartment but at the last minute, the condo failed an electrical inspection. I couldn't move in for another week and I was basically homeless. I asked my father if I could stay with him, and he happily agreed. He liked having his kids at home and I think if he

The Lonely Boy

could figure out a way to get me out of the contract altogether, he would have been happy to have me move back permanently. I was very good to him and we had dinner together every night that week.

Mary Anne and Norman had moved to Hillsborough after the wedding and rented a house but her job was still near my dad's house. On the way back from my closing she happened to be there when I came home with my closing papers. She never even acknowledged that I bought my first home. She just said, "I have to get back to work," and left. It would be almost a year before she even saw it. It didn't faze me through. It was just who she was and you couldn't miss something you never had. My dad helped me move and I was thrilled to start my life in a new town and a beautiful brand new condo.

I am someone who is very independent and motivated to achieve. If I say I am going to do something, I do it. I also realized early on that no one was going to help me in this life. If I wanted something I would have to make it happen myself. My mother's rejection made me strive harder to show her I could have a good life and make something of myself, even if it was after her death. I was determined to be successful and respected and honor her memory. It is something that still drives me today. One thing about my relationship with my mother was that she prepared me for her death and told me to honor my father and stay close to him and her family. I was determined to do that despite the many obstacles that would come my way.

In 1992, my maternal grandmother passed away. She had heart problems that led to a stroke. When my mom was diagnosed with cancer, they were afraid to tell grandma for fear of how her heart would react. My mother called her from the hospital bed as I watched. Mom told her she had not been in touch because she and my dad were away on a trip. Grandma would not find out about my mother's illness until after she was brain dead. When she went to see her daughter on the day before she died, my grandmother didn't even recognize her.

Sometime after my mom passed, grandma had heart surgery. She did well at first, but had a massive stroke while she was recuperating at home. The last years of her life were spent at home with an aide but there was nothing there. Mom's siblings did right by their mother and kept her at home. My Aunt Maria always made sure grandma was well taken care of. She did all the right things for her. For his part, Uncle Jack worked with the round-the-clock aides.

It was all very sad and now yet another loss for all of us. Aunt Maria and Uncle Jack decided it would be nice to buy a crypt in New Jersey near my mother's so mother and daughter could be together and they did just that. Then my Uncle Jack bought two more crypts because he decided he

The Lonely Boy

wanted to be buried next to my grandmother even though
my grandfather was still alive and they were still married.
They actually asked me if I would be buried with my
grandfather after he was gone, so Jack could be with my
grandmother. Do you see the dysfunction here? They were
always very loving but totally dysfunctional.

I told them I was very young and planned on having a full
life and someone to share it with. I told them to put
grandma and grandpa together as it should be and call it a
day. I guessed they assumed because I was gay I would be
alone my whole life.

Grandma and grandpa did not get along. When I came
down the stairs on the morning of my mother's funeral,
they were fighting with each other. I had to say something
to get them to stop. After the funeral they wanted to get a
divorce, but then she had the stroke. When grandma died,
my grandfather did not go to her funeral. It was a very
dysfunctional group.

Although I loved them very much and both grandparents
were extremely good to me. I was only out to my
immediate family and my mother's brother and sister at this
time. None of them took it very well or made it easy on me.
I decided to try to be the best I could be and show people
that my sexuality did not define me. It was just a single
facet of my existence. My mother's sister Maria really
stepped up after my mother died. She took mom's death
very hard and made every attempt to be close to all her

The Lonely Boy

sister's children. We saw Maria often in the years right after mom passed. She took over all the holidays and treated my dad like a brother, not a brother-in-law. She called me often and we became very connected. There was only one problem. She had studied with Jehovah's Witnesses and was not at all happy that I was gay. She was also mentally unstable and could be irrational at times. I will say that she had a good heart and when I needed her, she was always there for me. Maria was also quite bright and could be a great resource if you had a health problem.

I know she really wanted to connect with my sisters more. She made every attempt to get close to them as well as me, but as fate would have it, I was the one most like my mother with the warmth and compassion. The girls were not really interested and just went through the motions. Jennifer was immature and didn't understand the value of her aunt. Mary Anne simply didn't care. Mary Anne told me once in passing that Maria should be on medication for her issues. Mary Anne didn't respect her and I know that disappointed her. It is ironic that she and I had the relationship she really wanted with my sisters. That is the funny thing about life. Things don't always work out the way you think. We all are different. You just have to adapt to what you have been given.

The year that followed was a little lonely for me. I was living in a new town where I did not know anyone. I was dating but it never lead to anything long term and I was still

The Lonely Boy

very much in love with Brian. I knew he was living with someone else in the carriage house I used to live in with him. It broke my heart to think that someone was living my life. I am a true Taurus in that way: when I love someone, it is for life. I am very loyal and feel things very deeply. It's a good quality, but not always a healthy thing. I attribute a lot of my health problems to my feelings and my disappointments in life. I had been suffering with ulcerative colitis for a few years after my mom's death and the end of my relationship with Brian. I started on some new medications and had gone into remission. I was put on steroids for a short time and began to gain weight. For the first time in my life, I wasn't skinny anymore. I slowly went from 165 to about 195 pounds. I was 6'2" so I wasn't fat, but my body definitely changed and I was constantly trying to get the weight off. My father and mother were both extremely fit, and my dad was on me constantly about my weight gain. He was obsessed with thinness in everyone and only dated women who looked anorexic. He was a big eater but worked very hard and went dancing five nights a week. He remained very thin and young looking even as he was turning 60.

In December of 1992 my dad would turn 60. I decided I wanted to have a surprise party for him, and I called my sisters for help. Jennifer never got back to me and I had to call Mary Anne three times before she returned my call.

The Lonely Boy

There was a restaurant close to my condo in a little village. I got a great deal and asked Mary Anne to meet me there.

Unlike the first time, she did and I booked it. I handled all the details: I bought the invitations, the liquor, and decorations. I just asked her to address the invitations and to mail them. Two weeks before the party there were no responses. I started calling people and found out they never got the invitations. When I called Mary Anne, she said she gave them to her husband to mail but he never mailed them. She said it was an accident, but I knew he did it on purpose. Several people couldn't make it, since it was Christmas time and I was now calling at the last minute. But we had a good turnout anyway and my dad was really surprised.

The party was in the village where I lived and most people had never been to my new home. After the party, I invited everyone back to my condo but it was like pulling teeth. The only people who wanted to come back were the friends. My dad and the friends came back, the family went home. This started to become a pattern with my family. I was invited to all the family events, but no one ever wanted to come to my house. At first I was just disappointed, but over time it became very hurtful. If learned one thing from my mother's premature and sudden departure, it was that life is temporary and rites of passage are very important. I was going to celebrate everything because you never know what the future holds. To this day, I will never miss someone's birthday. I love connecting with people and making them feel special. Life is to be lived to the fullest, because we don't know what the future holds and you don't want any regrets. It was unfortunate that I was a part of a family that except for my dad just didn't get this. Every time I planned an event, they manufactured a problem or found a way not to be a part of it. It really disappointed me, and I think over time it led to my bouts of ill health.

In the spring of 1993, I was not feeling very well. I was now over 200 lbs. and had high blood pressure and a rapid heartbeat. I couldn't get the weight off and I was tired all the time. I went to the doctor and he sent me for tests. I found out I had a thyroid tumor. I truly believe that all my sadness led me to this. I have learned through my years that a tumor is nothing more than just concentrated sadness. I believe poor mental health has a lot to do with poor physical heath and I felt that was the reason it was happening to me.

Oddly enough it was my Aunt Maria, who would do anything she could to avoid coming to my home, who was the one who rushed to my side to help. Once, on the subject of coming to my home for a holiday, she once actually said, "If there's traffic on the bridge, we are just going to turn around and go home." Maria sent me to Mt. Sinai hospital in New York where I eventually had my surgery. I also went to Sloan Kettering for a second opinion. In those days, they did large needle biopsies and I had three painful biopsies through my neck. They thought the tumor was cancerous and set a date for surgery.

It was at this very time that I met John, the man who would become my long term partner. It's odd, on the Valentine's Day after Brian dumped me; I was in the city walking around alone. I was remembering the Valentine's Day dinner Brian made for me when we first met and I was distraught. I saw a sign for a psychic and spontaneously went in. I had never seen a psychic before and I was a little scared, but felt pulled in.

I remember the Empire State Building was all lit up in red for the holiday and it was very romantic as I was walking around. I went in very depressed because Brian had moved on with his life and I hadn't. I asked the psychic if I would ever find love again. She said I would meet someone with the initial "J" and we would be together for a long time.

It was a chance meeting that brought John and I together. I was meeting a friend of mine named Bill. Bill and I met in college and became good friends. Over the years we lost touch, but I had recently run into him twice and we decided to reconnect at a GAAMC (Gay Activist Alliance of Morris County) meeting. The group met on Monday nights and it was a great way to meet friends without going to a bar. One of the reasons Bill and I met there was because he had just taken a job in Manhattan and he was meeting a guy who was looking to rent a room to a commuter. That man turned out to be the "J" the psychic was talking about.

The Lonely Boy

I wasn't looking to meet someone at the time. I was actually seeing someone and was there with him when John and I met. When I first saw John, I felt a spark. An inner voice told me this guy would make a good partner.

John was very different from Brian. He was handsome, but shorter, graying, and a little overweight. Bill introduced us and I said hello. I introduced John to Steven, the man I was with. I actually thought he was a little short with me. The next time I saw Bill, he invited me to John's house. Bill ended up renting the room from John. John was throwing himself a birthday party. He owned a catering business and hosted parties all the time. I had broken up with Steven by now and I was free, so I went. I bought John a very nice bottle of wine and he opened it in front of me. He was a gracious host, but after he poured me a drink, I didn't see him again that night. Another man at the party took a liking to me and I spent the entire night talking to that guy on John's sun porch. As I went to say goodnight to John, I mentioned that my birthday was the very next day and that Bill and I and a group of guys from GAAMC were going to dinner. I invited him and he said yes. The next day came and went but he didn't show up or even call. I assumed he was just being polite that night, but I thought it was a little rude not to call. Imagine my surprise when Bill called me and told me John was interested in me. I told Bill to give him my number and he did. He called right away but it would be weeks before we actually went out. I was in

The Lonely Boy

and out of New York City hospitals with tests, and John was in high gear with spring weddings at his catering business. I explained that I had a thyroid tumor and I didn't know what was going to happen to me. I told him my mother died young and of cancer so I was concerned. We learned that both my mother and his brother died young and of leukemia. We talked about how that changed our lives and made us more aware of time and our mortality. I think that's when we bonded. We would speak every night for two to three hours for the next two weeks and we never ran out of anything to talk about.

On the night of our first date, we made plans to meet at his house. I got lost and was an hour late. Cell phones and navigation systems were not readily available back then and I had no way to reach him. John assumed I changed my mind and got changed for bed. When I finally showed up he seemed surprised but happy. He quickly changed and we were on our way. We had our first date in Manhattan. John was a native New Yorker and he knew the city very well. It was the perfect evening in June. We had dinner at a restaurant called Claire and then went to the Five Oaks to hear Marie Blake sing. We finally ended up in the village at an outdoor cafe for tiramisu at 2 am.

We were sitting in the courtyard when he said, "You are the one I am going to be with for the rest of my life."

"You don't know that," I said. I explained to him that I had a tumor and that I didn't know what was going to

The Lonely Boy

happen. Much to my surprise and unlike Brian, John stuck by me. He was the one to bring me to the hospital when I had surgery. When I was being admitted they asked John if he was a family member. He told them he was my partner. Back then, you didn't necessarily have the right to be there if you weren't family, but the nurse acknowledged John and it was fine. It was at that time that all worlds collided and my family met my boyfriend.

This was the first time anyone in the family was seeing me with another man, and if it weren't because I was going into surgery, I don't think they would have wanted to meet him. I went into surgery with John by my side. My dad was there, along with my Aunt Maria and Uncle Jack. Neither of my sisters ever showed. Some things never change.

I was in my hospital room overlooking Central Park with some of the most expensive views in Manhattan. I began to laugh as I was waiting for them to take me for surgery. It was ridiculous that I was sick. What I was really suffering from was a broken heart, not a broken thyroid. I decided that if I was ok afterwards, that I was going to give John a chance. I didn't have the same chemistry with him as I did Brian, but he was very special and I was going to try to finally move on.

Well, I made it through surgery. The doctors determined that the tumor did some damage but in the end it was benign. John had planned and paid for a week's vacation in

The Lonely Boy

Cape Cod before we ever met, so when he saw me after surgery and found out I was ok, he went on the trip he had planned and I went back to my father's house for a week.

As soon as John returned from the Cape he picked me up and took me home, to his house. I pretty much never left after that. I just started living with him because of the circumstances. He was so good to me and so nurturing. He also had a dog named Cajun that I fell in love with. Except for the short period of time that dog wandered into our yard after my mother's death, I never experienced a pet. This dog was so sweet; I just fell in love with him. He was a comfort to me and we bonded when John was working and I was at home recuperating with Cajun. When I eventually returned to my job, John's house was much closer to my work. I had terrible fatigue and being close really helped a great deal. He came into my life at just the right time. I always wondered if my mom had something to do with the timing of it.

Now that I was going to be all right and my family met John, things softened a bit with them. They were so pleased that I didn't have cancer; I think they let their guard down a bit. They slowly began accepting John into my life, even though I know they weren't happy about it. I kept my condo in Bedminster, but John was renting in a large ranch house in Roseland, New Jersey and we basically lived there. It was close to work and close to the city and we used to go in often.

The Lonely Boy

1994 brought record snowfalls and we spent lots of nights in front of the fireplace. It was a good year for us. Bill was still renting the extra room and it was nice to spend time with him again. We fixed him up with a friend of mine named David and they quickly became our new go-to couple socially. John had his own group of friends and some of them were very nice to me. Michael was very sweet and reached out to me right away. He and John had gone to the Culinary Institute together and had been friends for many years. He was warm and I felt he was like a family cousin right from the start. In later years he really became an important and meaningful part of our lives. Tom was really funny and would make me laugh. I really liked him too. Tom had a young boyfriend named Roland. He was really sweet, but he was so much younger than the rest of us, we liked to tease him a bit. The girls, Glen Ellen and Michelle, were also nice and we spent a lot of time with them too. Finally there was Albert. He and John had spent a great deal of time together before John met me. I think he resented our relationship and as a result he was never all that nice to me. But we were part of a pretty big group of friends and there was always a great deal to do.

There were a lot of good things about being closer to Manhattan. The restaurants were better and there were more services and shopping. John was a city person and he showed me new things I never saw before. He made me more sophisticated. He was also very warm and I felt very safe with him. I was not at my best when we first met but he stuck by me and I grew to love him. Whenever there were family functions now it was Rich and John together and I liked the new dynamic. They were a little more respectful to me now that there was another person in the mix. Even Mary Anne came around a little bit. I was hoping this would be the beginning of a new chapter with my family.

In the fall of 1994 Mary Anne announced that she was going to have a baby. After my nephew was born, all events moved to my sister's house. Norman told the family when we were in Brooklyn at Maria's house that he was not coming there again. Norman wanted everything on his own turf and once baby Michael was born everything changed. I will say this was the one period of time Mary Anne tried to connect with me. Much to my surprise, she asked me to be the baby's godfather. I was shocked but very happy. All I ever wanted was acceptance and the love of my family. But those with the children hold all the cards, and Norman was now in charge. I had to realize that despite the snide comments and the little things he would do and say, I would have to ignore them if I wanted a family. I'd just have to bite my tongue.

When little Mikey was born, I was so excited I left my job in the middle of the day and I stopped to get Mary Anne a bouquet of daffodils. I double-parked to get them and got a parking ticket. He was born in April just like me,

The Lonely Boy

right before my 30th birthday. I was crazy about this kid but always concerned that things would change with Norman as his dad.

Two weeks later I would turn 30, and I told John I didn't want a party. He threw me a surprise 29th the previous year and I hid in the bathroom after I saw all the guests. I hate change and I hate surprises, just as my parents did. We had a quiet dinner for this birthday and that was perfect for me. In November of that year, my Aunt Maria took a fall down the stairs and got hurt. She was in the hospital and we went to visit her. I took the bus into New York, and John picked me up at a bar near his work hours later. He was very late and I wound up having two drinks with no food in me. I was a little buzzed when we arrived. After we visited with Aunt Maria, my uncle took John aside and suggested I had a drinking problem. To the Irishman that I was with, that was very funny.

The next week was Thanksgiving, and because I knew Maria wouldn't travel in the best of times, John and I brought her an entire Thanksgiving dinner—everything from soup to nuts with plenty of leftovers so there would be food in the house. While we were eating, John mentioned that he hired disabled people to give them a sense of independence. He had a mentally challenged dishwasher named Patrick who was very sweet and a good worker. Somehow Maria got it into her head that he was employing people with AIDS and that they had cooked her food. The next day, she called and accused us of poisoning her and her family with AIDS food. I was so upset, I hung up. I didn't know how to respond. After that I took a bit of a hiatus from Aunt Maria. When her daughter graduated from high school, we decided we wouldn't go to the graduation party, but Maria's daughter was my mother's godchild and I didn't want to take it out on her. I went to Tiffany & Company and had a necklace made with a locket. In the locket was my mother's picture. In her card, I wrote about the day she was born and how excited my mother was that she had a beautiful baby girl as her godchild. I handed my dad the gift and card so he could bring it to the party. He said, "You are not just good, you are too good." I never received a response or a thank you card.

In 1996, John and I hit our three year mark and we decided we wanted to buy a house together. He wanted to live in the city. I wanted to live in Bedminster, in a real house with a pool. We looked in the city and I rode the subway for the first time. New York was still affordable back then and we could have bought a small one bedroom apartment for $300,000 in a decent area. I am not a city boy. I hated public transportation and I was not going to a laundromat. New York felt like a giant step backwards to me back then. Bedminster was country. It was beautiful and clean and new. I could keep my car and I felt safe and comfortable there. John liked the development I lived in

The Lonely Boy

and they were still building so we looked at new homes and townhouses in my area. We eventually bought one. Today, I realize we made a mistake and I blame myself for it. We would have done much better in the city. My career would be further along and we would have made a killing in real estate. I just wasn't ready for such a change. Change is extremely hard for me and always will be. My parents were very conservative and creatures of habit and so am I. It's funny how when we get older we become like our parents. As I age, I look into the mirror and I'm starting to see my father both in my habits and in my appearance. My dad built a new colonial and that's exactly what I wanted.

We were living at the time in a large ranch in Roseland. John wanted to buy it, and he asked me to buy it with him. John was working in the city. It was close to New York and we could be in Manhattan in 20 minutes. I agreed and we met with the owner and made a formal offer. We were going to put in a second floor and I had some great plans for the conversion. It wasn't exactly what I wanted, but John had been so good to me I was ready to compromise. The Roseland area was nice, but Bedminster was picturesque and pristine, back then even more so than today. We went down to see the owner, Mrs. MacClellen, in her retirement village and presented our offer. She had recently lost her husband and she didn't want to keep the property. We presented our offer along with a promise to maintain the property and love it. The property had been left to her son who died tragically at 18. She held onto it for over 30 years for sentimental reasons. She told us that the funeral director around the corner also wanted the property and was going to make an offer as well. We told her he was planning to tear the house down to add parking for his business and cautioned her not to sell to him. In the end, we didn't get the house. When she died shortly after, he did exactly what we said he would. He paved our paradise and put up a parking lot. I went to see it once and it was very sad. It made it very clear to me that nothing lasts forever and you need to enjoy the moments when you are in them.

With that news in hand, we decided to head for The Hills and buy a new townhouse in my complex. John moved out of the ranch on Memorial Day weekend with Cajun in tow and the three of us lived together in my 1,000 square foot condo until the townhouse was finished in September.

On moving day, my dad and John were instrumental in getting things done. I couldn't get off work and the two of them bonded. It was nice to see how well they worked together. Unlike Brian, who dad hated for hurting me, John was a good man and he respected him. We settled into our new house and became friends with our neighbors. John and I did a lot of entertaining and it was a very social time for us. There were lots of dinners out and our new neighbors quickly became friends. This was a very good time for us. John and I joined Weight Watchers together and John lost a great deal of weight. He was in a good place. We were young and happy and he loved his job. One day I drove home and saw him talking on our front lawn to a neighbor. He was actually slim now. He looked so good I couldn't believe it. This didn't last though and quickly he gained back the 30 pounds he lost plus more. We both love food and have had a lifelong struggle with food versus self esteem. John never was slim again but I ping-ponged from being too thin to being chubby and back to being thin from that time on. John's job was now in Long Island City and he had to be at the train before 6 am. I felt sorry for him but he loved his work and talked about it all the time. I was still in the hotel business, and had been offered a new position at a larger airport hotel. I took it and got a big bump up in my salary. The job required a great deal of travel. I was negotiating with airlines and their crews. So I got a huge amount of perks and John and I took advantage of all of them. I also was in better mental health then.

An opportunity came up for me to go to Los Angeles right before Christmas. I really wanted to go, but John couldn't get time off from work. I flew out alone and met one of my friends there. I don't think I would ever do that today. I am now too co-dependent. My friend and I did a lot of great and touristy things while we were in L.A. John felt I was safe with him because he was much more street smart than I was. I went to a taping of a television talk show and got to be on camera. In the years to follow, I would go to California three or four more times, but this was my first time and it was very exciting. I was a little naïve about how dangerous L.A. was though. One day when my friend and I were driving our rental car, a guy tried to carjack us at a traffic light. He came up to me in the passenger side window and made it seem like he had a gun. He told us get out of the car. My friend reacted very quickly—he hit the gas and we sped off. It scared us so much that we left L.A. early and drove to San Diego.

San Diego was much quieter and seemed safer. It was very pretty and the weather was great. It was so strange being in southern California at Christmas. All the trees were flocked and poinsettias were planted in pots outside and in the center medians of the streets. I think the gay area there is called the Hillcrest section. We spent a lot of time there because my friend was single. One night we were in a bar and a young blond man started talking to me. He told me he had been in the military. He was very pleasant and we were just talking. All of a sudden a Filipino guy with glasses came over to me and punched me really hard in the arm. I was stunned. My friend grabbed me and we got out of there fast. My friend was very street smart and he said he saw crazy in this guy's eyes. A year later, I saw the same guy on the news. He was serial killer Andrew Cunanan from San Diego. He killed the man I was talking to that day along with Gianni Versace and many others. He finally shot himself to death in Miami after a manhunt for him. Life is so unpredictable.

The Lonely Boy

John and I traveled often and I began to get over my fear
of flying. Kiwi Airlines was one of my accounts then and
every time they opened up a new run we were on the first
flight. We went to Bermuda, Puerto Rico, and Florida and
took many trips to warmer climates at this time.

In 1997, John became dissatisfied with the board in our
homeowners association and ran for a position. He won the
election and he and I founded a social committee. We
planned clubhouse parties, trips and great activities. One
that stands out was a summer barbeque we hosted. It was
very upscale with filet mignon and fresh flowers. John went
around selling tickets. When he rang one woman's doorbell
she said, "Do you have a child?" When he said no, she then
asked, "Do you want one?" She invited him in for a glass
of wine and he went in. Her name was Marie and she and
her husband eventually became not just our best friends,
but actually family to us. At the end of 1997, my airport
hotel was sold and the entire staff was herded into a room
and let go. I was shocked but that's how hotels work. They
like to bring their own people in.

I decided after 10 years in the hotel industry, I wanted to
something more stable. I stayed in sales but started looking
for a business-to-business opportunity. Now at 32, I wanted
something that would offer more of a sense of permanence.
I had finally gotten the travel bug out of my system.

I wound up taking a sales job for a large corporation.
There was a lot of training at the beginning and I was away

The Lonely Boy

for several weeks. I immediately noticed this line of work was much more conservative. I was the only one in my group who wasn't married. I was worried I wouldn't fit in and at first it was very awkward. My boss asked me about my personal life on my last interview. I was vague, but I knew he knew. There were no rights for gay people then and I felt I had to be discreet. I got the job, but the guy was a gossip and I overheard people talking about the new guy being gay before they even met me. I tried to keep a low profile and most people were very nice to me, but there was a guy there that was difficult and over time it became a problem. Mary Alice, a colleague of mine, picked up on the discord and started having lunch with me. The team kind of broke up into two groups and even though it was never discussed, I knew the reason. Every time there was a trip, I had a hotel room to myself even though everyone else had to share, even my own boss. It made me feel really bad, but I was doing well at the job so I stayed on and kept my personal business personal.

I remember this being a particularly good time between John and I relationship-wise. We were both in sync and both happy at the same time. Depression was nowhere in sight and this period would be my longest stretch of good mental health.

As much as I loved our new friends, I was growing tired of living in a planned community. I wanted a larger home with a pool and we started looking. I have always been very

93

The Lonely Boy

ambitious. It might be and oldest child thing, but I feel the need to succeed and to continually prove myself.

The real estate market was exploding at the time and you didn't even need a realtor to sell a house in our area. You just put a sign out on your lawn and the offers came rolling in. On the buying side, however, we hated everything we looked at. I had started doing a little interior design work on the side in addition to my corporate job and we got a taste of wealth. I wanted the dream house, but we weren't there yet. I think John was very content where we were, but I pushed him to grow and he was very accommodating to help me make my dreams come true.

In an ironic twist of fate it was my sister's husband Norman who suggested that we look for a lot and build. We had been through at least a hundred resale homes and there was nothing that met our expectations. One day we took a ride further west and hit on a little town called Tewksbury. It was a charming old world village and very much out in the country. It was horse country and there were no conveniences nearby, but it was stunningly beautiful. We spent every weekend looking for land and took my dad with us. Dad was going to advise us since this was our first building project. We were both very eager, but very green. When I saw our lot on Rocky Glen Way, I immediately knew I wanted it. It was four acres with views on a very prestigious street. We made a low offer and it was accepted. I sold our townhouse in one day for $30,000

The Lonely Boy

more than the bank-appraised value and we moved out
quickly with no place to go.

The Lonely Boy

Chapter 7   Pulling a Joe Ballopkins

For the first 21 years of my life I did not truly know my father. Sure, he was always there, but my mom ruled the roost and he was happy with that. The only non-horrific post-mom experience was that I was now getting to know my father.

Dad is a very good man. He was a good son, a patient husband and a loyal friend. Dad, however, was often a difficult man. When he was a little boy there was a tragedy in the house that resulted in a great deal of attention on his family. Also, his parents never spoke a word of English. I surmise that these things had left him and probably his brother a little isolated. I don't think he got the socialization in his early years that he needed.

His brother Joe fared a little better. Joe had Phil and she was very good for him. They built a great and long life together and were very successful. My mom and dad quarreled often but my dad will tell you the best part of his life was when he had his young family under his roof. He told me once, "It was the best time in my life." How could you not love him for that? He was also very loyal to my mom. He dated in the years after she passed away but he never got close to anyone again. I think that's why I care about him so much. He is very loyal. He should have gotten married again though. He thrived with a woman in his life.

The Lonely Boy

Dad needed direction. His early years on Clifton Avenue were productive because he had a guiding force behind him. In the years that came after he didn't fare as well. He had a lot of anger and became bitter. I will say he did adapt to his new role of having to cook and clean much better than I thought he would. On Jen's first day back to school after the funeral, he made her scrambled eggs in a saucepan but by the end of the first year he had become a pretty good cook. He used to take a pineapple and quarter it very artfully. He would make the four sections into boats and top each section with strawberries. This was his signature healthy dessert. He made John and I eggplant one night and it was so good I asked him what his secret was? He said that he made it with love. You can't beat that.

On the other hand, he could also be very cruel and critical. He would often say and do things that were inappropriate for a father. It was never mean-spirited, he just didn't have the best communication skills and he wasn't up on accepted protocol, especially without a wife's guidance. I don't mean to bash my father. He loved his kids, but he never really took over as the leader. I needed him to step up and he never really did.

One of the first times I noticed this was when I started working in the hotel business. In addition to your regularly scheduled hours, on a rotating basis you had "MOD duty" and as the "Manager on Duty" you had to stay in the hotel overnight and act as the onsite supervisor. It didn't happen

The Lonely Boy

all the time, but when you were on duty, you were basically locked in the building for 24 straight hours.

Whenever I had MOD duty I would always invite dad for dinner. It was a nice free meal for him and we would get to talk. When the 1990s rolled around my hotel brought in country line dancing. I invited him to come and he always did. Dad was a great dancer and he eventually went out dancing five nights a week in the years after my mom died. It was his socialization in the evenings after his long and lonely days. I introduced him to a few people and before I knew it he was gone. He disappeared onto the dance floor and I didn't see him again that night. He didn't even come up to my office to say good night or thank you. This happened a lot with dad. He also never remembered my birthday. In later years, John would call to remind him and he would always tell me that John told him to call.

Dad was also tight with the buck. As soon as I started working, I paid everywhere we went. I even paid for his youngest daughter's Sweet 16 Party. I once spent the day with him in Sloan Kettering where I was having tests for my thyroid tumor. He took me for spaghetti afterwards and when check came he told me, "You owe me 8 bucks." Dad was not a sport. When I turned 40, he came to the party and said, "I didn't feel the need to get you anything."

I know he was proud of me but he could have been a little more generous and caring especially because he was the sole parent now. I always cut him a break though, because he was a widower. On one occasion however it really got to me.

In 1989 I got my real estate license. I was very ambitious and had great plans for the future. I started looking at investment properties. My original plan was to purchase a two-family house. I would live on the first floor and rent out the upper floor to help pay the mortgage, just as my grandparents had done. I eventually found a property I liked and took my father to see it. When I showed it to him he like it so much, he tried to bid on it for himself. Neither one of us got it though—a restaurateur bought it.

I then began to show him other income properties in New Brunswick. I said, "Now that you're getting older, you need to think about retirement income." He agreed and became very interested. In the end, he called me one day and told me he looked at a property without me. He used the listing realtor and I received no commission, not even a referral fee. This is what John and I refer to as "pulling a Joe Ballopkins." Joe was the real estate agent dad used. There were a whole host of crappy little things a father should never do to his kids. It was never evil. He just was clueless. He didn't know any better. In truth, dad was not really the father I needed. He was not strong and when problems occurred with my sisters he never backed me. I often think he put his needs ahead of mine and I resented it. I will say though that I always felt loved by him, and whenever there was a crisis he wouldn't walk, he would run to be there for me. Part of my own growth as a person was being able to understand this and love him in spite of his flaws. I realize he didn't sign up for a gay son either. I'm sure that it wasn't easy for him, but he never let me see that. He was actually pretty accepting. I found out once that he went out on a double date with a friend of mine and his male partner. They were trying to set him up with his partner's mom. He had no qualms about it. He would often show up at my house unexpectedly with a date in tow. I always loved that he felt comfortable enough with me to do that. Once we were having a party with four other gay couples. He stopped by with a new gal and stayed for dinner. I think it was their first date!!!

I don't think it ever dawned on him that some of these women might be uncomfortable with my sexuality. He just accepted me for who I was and I was lucky to have that. That's the thing about life. Things don't always work out the way you plan. Like a tree that blows in the wind, you have to bend a bit if you want to survive.

That part of life I think he understood. In spite of my frustrations with dad we stayed very close and I am glad I have the memories of those days to draw upon. He once said to me in passing, "I know you would never walk away from me no matter what." And I never have.

The Lonely Boy

Chapter 8   Go West Young Men

It was 1999 and the economy was booming. We now owned a four acre lot on a hill with views, but we had no place to live. We tried to find a temporary apartment but none were available at the time. We decided to live with our families until the house was completed. I moved in with my father, and John moved in with his sister.

Thank God for our friends though. We used to spend weekends together at our friend Gerard's house. Gerard had gone to the Culinary Institute with John. About a year after I met John, they ran into each other and John invited Gerard to dinner. Gerard arrived in skin-tight clothes, and my radar immediately began pinging. I was enraged. I said, "Who is this guy and what is he looking for? Get rid of him. No one wears jeans that tight unless they're looking for something."

Well, we had dinner and by the end of the night Gerard and I were doing all the talking. John went to bed, since he had to be up at 5 am the next morning for work. Gerard and I stayed up and talked for another hour. I really liked this guy. Like me, his mother died of cancer and he had unresolved issues with her too. He also had suffered with the same self esteem issues I did. When John and I moved in together into our townhouse in Bedminster, Gerard followed us soon after. We found him a condo in our development. By letting us stay with him in our old

The Lonely Boy

neighborhood, Gerard really helped us feel grounded even without a house to go to.

Marie and Ross also stepped in at this time. Marie cooked for us every Sunday night and they became our second family. It was the first time we were living apart since we met. John wasn't out to his family yet and it complicated things a great deal. In retrospect, I don't know why we didn't live together at my father's house during construction. I know dad would have loved having us there and having John cook for him. But at the time, Jennifer was still living with dad. Her boyfriend Mark and Jen's friend Kim were living there too. It was a full house.

My dad was acting as our general contractor and the three of us would meet each night to discuss what had happened at the construction site. John and I found ways to be together and somehow that worked for us then. I can't see that working now. We are both far too co-dependent, and I need companionship to keep my depression in check. But at the time, it was just what we had to do. We were taking on a lot and got scared when we realized we gave up something that was working for us. We were also completely green about building a home and my dad often gave us cause for concern in his judgment about dealing with the subcontractors. But we loved the new area and would bring friends to the construction site on weekends to show them our progress.

The Lonely Boy

This was also a very happy time in our lives. I liked connecting with my dad and he was happy we were moving into a home with a lot of property. He liked the area so much that several years later he started looking for land where he could build a house for his retirement nearby. Things were also going well for John and I at work. John had been transferred to New Jersey so his daily commute was much more manageable now and my sales career was really starting to take off.

My sister Mary Anne and my nephew came to the job site one day and we showed them what we were doing. It was a cold day in December. I ran out and got hot chocolate and donuts for them. We sat in my car and ate them. I was so happy. I loved my sisters and wanted to be closer to them. This was a rare occasion and I was hopeful about the future.

Unfortunately, as fate would have it, we started having problems with the construction. We were building on a hill and our excavation costs were skyrocketing. We also had to put in a very complicated and costly septic system and we were way over budget. At one point we were out of money on our construction loan. You only get money in installments with a construction loan and we were out of cash.

We were going to have to take out a personal loan until my dad stepped in. He said he would loan us the money in the interim. We were paying my father every week for his work. We were also paying his expenses and feeding him. I guess he felt it was his job to help us just as he had helped both of my sisters at times along the way.

Dad wrote a note for a $20,000 temporary loan that we all signed. Within a month, we had our next installment and we wrote him a check for the full amount. Dad said, "No. Give me half and float the other half 'til we finish construction so we don't have this problem again." So that's exactly what we did. He was right and we faced several more shortages until we got our CO.

Shortly before we got the green light to move in, my dad called my sister's husband Norman to the house. He had gotten into the habit of borrowing my father's tools and not returning them. We were doing finish trim work and dad needed his tools. Norman showed up at the house with a friend of his. This was the guy who was his best man years earlier. The friend was raving about our street and how nice it was. Norman was not happy. He walked through the house and knocked everything we did. He was a real low-life, so I expected that of him. My dad once told me that Norman borrowed some of his tools, sold them, and kept the money. It was a precursor to what would come to be a major tragedy and the undoing of my father in later years. Norman left in a huff.

The following week I received an email from my sister about St. Patrick's Day dinner. Our mom died on March 18th, the day after St. Patrick's Day. In the subsequent years we started all having dinner together to remember her. It was odd, an Italian family celebrating St. Patrick's Day, but we were starting to act like a family again and I was happy to go. I was angry at her husband for knocking our new home, but I let it go, as I always did, to have a relationship with my nephew. My dad decided not to go. It was just the six of us, my two sisters, Norman, John, me and my young nephew.

We were having a nice time telling stories about mom. Mom had always been obsessed with her slimness and her age. She once said to me, "Don't ever get a girl pregnant because I'll be a grandmother too early and people will think I'm older than I am." We were wondering how she would have handled telling people she was a grandmother now. We were all laughing about that and I guess Norman felt left out. I added that when I started maturing my mother once said, "You're too grown up to be my son." Norman turned to me and told me she was denying being my mother because she was embarrassed of who I was. I looked at this turd with disgust and thought, "OMG. THIS IS IT. I AM DONE." I decided not to make a scene in front of my very young nephew, but this time he went too far. He never even met my mother and if she was alive, HE would have never been in the picture.

A week passed and the more I thought about it the angrier I became. The following week was my nephew's birthday and Mary Anne again sent an email inviting to us to come over for cake. This time I responded by calling. I called her and told her I was very unhappy at what her husband said. She cried for a moment then hung up. It would never be the same again. There were no more emails after that. No more invites, it was over.

As always, she was just going through the motions for her son. There was never any love in anything she did with me. She never once picked up the phone to call me. You would get a group email to her command performances on her terms. If you didn't fit into her agenda, you didn't get a second thought. My sister Jennifer said Mary Anne once told her, "If I have to choose between my husband and my brother, I choose my husband." What a sick thought! I am sure he was putting pressure on her to get me out of their lives. The thought that someone would do that to their spouse speaks volumes for how little he loved her. This started a new phase in our family dynamic that would never get better and eventually lead to terrible tragedy.

My dad wasn't there that night but was very unhappy when he found out about it. Dad, himself, once told me that my mother didn't love me and that broke my heart. My mom didn't accept my lifestyle and we never had a chance to make it right. I have lived my whole life broken by the fact that we never had the chance to make peace. This worthless, jealous asshole was not going to degrade me or my relationship with my mother, especially not in front of his young son.

The Lonely Boy

Norman had a history of problems with people. He was mean-spirited and abusive. I remember one Christmas, my sister was crying because she said he never did anything to help her. I'm sure it was a very unhappy marriage and I was sad for her, but this guy had hit a nerve and I couldn't let it go.

I know my mother loved me, but the sense of loss I felt was over whelming. This guy was abusive and I wasn't going to take it anymore. I didn't raise my voice or yell at my sister. I just asked that he apologize. He refused.

He hated the idea that John and I were happy and that we could actually do well in life. He had to find a way to destroy it and keep his son away from us and this was it. When Michael was born he looked like my sister. He had the sweet little cleft chin just like hers. When he became a toddler, he started to look a lot like me. I even heard Norman say once to her, "OMG, he looks just like your brother." I think it really scared him. Michael was also very sweet. We he started nursery school a teacher told them to toughen him up a little. I think those two things coupled with the fact that John and I were making a real life together put him over the edge. We all knew from the beginning that this guy was trouble, but now there was no going back and as time went on it would only get worse.

In June of 1999, I was at work and a call came in to set up a new client at Caldwell Airport. It was not in my territory, but because I was in the office at that moment, my boss handed the lead to me. I went that afternoon and the man was very nice to me. He said, "If you have a moment, I'd like to show you something." He took me to a really beautiful small plane. He let me get in the pilot's seat and feel the interior. It was beautifully finished. He told me the plane belonged to someone who was very famous, but he couldn't tell me who it was. Two weeks later as I was watching the news, I heard that JFK Jr.'s plane was missing. When they showed the airport and the plane, it was the one I was just sitting in. My life, for some reason, has always brought me to strange circumstances. I have always wondered about the lesson in all of this. Was God trying to tell me something? It did shake me though and I realized even more how precious life is. I was not going to wait for things to happen because you just never know what life will bring next.

In March of 2000, we moved into our new house. We were house poor, but really happy to be done. In Tewksbury, people have a tradition of naming their homes. Often you will see little sign that says "River House" or "Applewood Farm." I wanted the perfect name for our modest home and then it came to me. The reason John and I connected was because of the two angels who brought us together, my mom Maryann and John's brother Vincent. I took the "Ma" from Maryann and the "Vin" from Vincent and came up with Mavin which means expert in Yiddish

The Lonely Boy

(though in Yiddish it's spelled "maven"). We built on a large hill so the property became Mavin Hill. We both loved it. John and I made a small oval sign in black and gold with that name and planted it in the ground at the entrance. We planned an elaborate housewarming party for that fall and I invited my sister and her husband. I waited most of the day to do the toast so we could tell the Mavin Hill story. I wanted Mary Anne to be there. I eventually gave up and did the dedication without her. There wasn't a dry eye in the house. It was perfect.

The Mavin Hill name has continued to bring us good fortune. It became more of a brand for me over time and brought me much success and happiness. Mary Anne never responded to our invitation and didn't show up 'til the end of the day. When she did, it was without her husband, and she brought no gift or card. I could tell she was unhappy, but I was glad she was there. It would be the last time she ever came to my home again.

She continued to host dinner for all the holidays but I was no longer welcome. Because she was the one with the children, my family all went there. Everyone in the family eventually learned about what was said at the St. Patrick's Day dinner and that Normal had refused to apologize. After all, it accomplished what he wanted it to. He got me out of the picture and his life went on with him in control.

But my dad was sick about it. He tried to talk to them but it was hopeless. I was really missing my nephew and for

The Lonely Boy

the next few years I would continue to drop off gifts at their mailbox or have my dad bring the gifts. Dad was losing his family and just as my mother had done; in trying times he went to the church for some answers. In the past, my mother handled all the family matters. Now that she was long gone, it was up to him to fix this. His current parish priest, not the one that molested me, suggested a family therapist. My dad resisted at first, but in time he eventually called her and booked an appointment for all of us.

My relationship with Jennifer also had been deteriorating after the split with Mary Anne. I resented the fact that she didn't support me and that she spent every holiday with my nephew and now a new niece. She spoke of them often to me. She didn't understand how lost I felt without them. One Father's Day I invited my dad, Jennifer and Mark, Jennifer's live-in boyfriend, over for dinner. Jen said that they could only come for breakfast because Mary Anne had a whole day planned. When they got to my house she rushed me to get out as soon as they ate. I told her dad was my father too and this was awful for me. She left in a huff. She couldn't understand my pain.

Jennifer was very immature and was in no rush to leave the nest. It took her over six years to get a four-year college degree. She didn't cook or clean for my father even after her boyfriend moved in. Jen was a grown up kid living at home with no responsibility. My dad even allowed my sister's boyfriend to move in with them. To ensure propriety, Mark lived in the basement.

On the bright side, Mark was nothing like Norman. He was sweet and he really loved Jen. He was not very ambitious though and I worried that Jennifer would not have a good life. Jen was not maturing and she was holding my dad back from living his own life. The best thing for Dad would have been to marry again. It wouldn't be easy for us to adjust to this, but he needed a wife. Jennifer tied him to the house and to an old life that was no longer fulfilling for him. He wanted her to move out, but she wasn't going anywhere. Mark and Jennifer even lived with dad after they were married. My father had to finally kick them out.

Mark once said he would be happy spending the rest of his life at 21 Clifton Avenue. I was very torn about that. I was happy my dad wasn't alone, but my sister was not taking care of him. He was getting older and he needed to find happiness again. Jennifer was holding him back and he used to complain to me about it. Unlike Mary Anne, who was gone for good, Jen and I continued to see each other. I was very good to her. I took her on a trip to Florida when I won the President's Circle award for excellence at work. I invited her and her husband over often. I bought her groceries and paid every time we went somewhere.

The Lonely Boy

I was there for Jen no matter what. I often felt, though, that she never appreciated it. As time went on we grew apart. She would spend all of her free time at Mary Anne's and would tell me what the kids were doing. I don't think she realized how it was tearing me apart inside. At some point, dad decided to get us all together in a room to talk. He arranged and paid for a neutral therapist to try to make us a family again. It was a disaster. First of all Norman did not show up. He got what he wanted, which was me booted from my family for good.

In the therapist's office, Mary Anne, Jen, Mark, Dad, John and I were all in the same room for the first time in a long time. Jennifer had become much closer to Mary Anne and was babysitting the kids. Jennifer, Mark and Mary Anne arrived together. It was a statement of solidarity. They began to act as one united front. At first the therapist talked and then we began to talk. My dad expressed his desire for us to be a family again. He also mentioned that it was quite obvious that Norman did not care to fix a thing and that's why he didn't show up. I said that I resented them being together without me and the fact that they thought it was ok. I brought up Father's Day when they rushed out by 10 am to spend the day as a family without me.

Mark chimed in and told me not to upset his girlfriend. It got heated and no one heard each other. Mark was living at my father's house for free and I told him I resented him chiming in. I wanted this to be a positive experience not a fighting session. Immature Jennifer and Mark got up and left with Mary Anne. It was over.

The next week my dad and I went back to therapist alone. She said it was obvious that Mary Anne did not want to reconcile and that we needed to get used to the fact that we would never be a family in the same way again. I wanted my father to step up and take charge himself, but he was weak. I also knew he was afraid they would drop him the way they dropped me and he couldn't handle not seeing his grandchildren. He and I continued going to therapy to try to deal with the new reality, but it was really sad for both of us. At about this same time, I started having anxiety attacks.

I had my first when I was with John on a trip to Washington DC. My old friend Rick had moved to Baltimore and we stopped to see him on the way. He was not doing well and had gotten involved with a young man who had been lying about his age. The boy's father was a cop and when he found out, Rick was arrested. He was living in a small room in a rough area and I was so worried about him. He had also developed a heart issue that he inherited from his mom and was on a lot of medication. That night, when John and I were having dinner, my heart started racing. We paid the check and when I stepped out of the restaurant into the cold air, I collapsed on the sidewalk. When I came to, I thought I'd had a heart attack. John put me into the car and I began to feel better. The next morning we went to an Urgent Care facility and my EKG showed no issues. I love very deeply and when I see someone in pain it affects me profoundly. It probably makes me a nice person, but it's not really a good thing for my health. When we got back from the trip, my regular physician put me on a medication for panic attacks. Mary Alice from work noticed I was not acting quite right one day and she called me on it. I told her I was on medication. I stopped the medication soon afterwards and the panic attacks eventually stopped. I thought maybe it was just a fluke or a food allergy to something I ate that night. I moved forward with my life after that with sadness but no fear. I was depressed, but the anxiety subsided for a while.

Jennifer and I reconciled after a couple of meetings alone at a bookstore of her choice, and when she and Mark planned to get married they made sure I was included in everything. I really liked Mark. He came from a broken home and was really in need of some TLC. Jennifer wasn't nurturing and she really wasn't right for him. I saw that when we were all living together while my house was being built. She would boss him around and yell at him. She would go out with her friends on weekends and leave him home alone, but he still loved her. When they married I feared it wouldn't last, but I never said a word. After what had happened with Mary Anne, I was content with the little family interaction I had left. Jennifer had learned from

The Lonely Boy

Mary Anne's poor choices, so this time John and I were invited to Mark's bachelor party. I was in the wedding party and John did one of the readings. Mary Anne was the Matron of Honor and we spent the entire day sitting next to each other without a word between us. It was so wrong and so sad that the man she married had destroyed our family, but he did. When my cousin Joey and his wife came to the head table to say goodnight they only acknowledged Mary Anne and Norman and then they walked out. I guess I wasn't really missing anything after all. My cousin Mary Jo, however, said she was going to invite us to her shore house while Jennifer was on her honeymoon. She called Mary Anne and asked her to contact me. Mary Anne emailed me at my work address knowing I was on vacation that week. When my out-of-office message came up she ignored it. She never called my home, my cell phone or contacted me at my home email. She made sure I didn't get to go. When Mary Anne and her family got there, Mary Jo told me later that Mary Anne said, "I don't know what my brother does." Mary Anne was a crafty bitch with no conscience. I needed family and I really wanted to be there.

Not much changed after Jen and Mark got back from their honeymoon. They still lived with dad and Jen often went out without her husband. It was like she still wanted to be a kid. I felt that maybe mom's early death scarred her so much she didn't want to leave the little girl role. When mom died, dad couldn't bring himself to tell Jen. He wasn't strong enough. He made me do it. Mary Anne was nowhere to be found. When I told her, Jen said, "I'm just a little girl. I am not ready to lose my mother." She then grabbed a picture of mom held it to her chest and ran to her bedroom in tears. She tucked that picture of mom under the glass on her chest of drawers where it stayed for many years. I still think of how tough that moment was. Maybe the pain kept her from maturing.

Over time, she started doing odd things. She started hanging out with another guy after she was married. This man bought her a truck. She became moody and distant. We didn't understand what was going on, and John and I began to wonder where her head was at. It was around this time my dad came to me and told me he wanted her out of the house. He gave them notice and they bought a sweet Cape Cod house in Manville near Mary Anne.

Around this same time, Jen starting having health problems and I became quite concerned. A doctor thought she might have an autoimmune disease like scleroderma. I read everything I could about it and I took her to the doctor myself even though she had a husband. It was unclear what was going on, but everyone seemed to notice a sharp change in her. My dad thought she might be bipolar. My Aunt Maria told me Jennifer could turn on a dime and be very nasty.

The Lonely Boy

I began to see a girl I did not recognize. She was always beautiful, but full figured. She had a dramatic weight loss now and always seemed angry when I saw her.

She decided to leave Mark and soon the marriage was over. With no warning, she dropped me too. No fight, no drama, she just stopped talking to me. I was so sad now that both girls were gone. As I have said, in my core the most important thing to me are family and good friends. I now only had my dad left. It broke both our hearts but we began to accept our new reality. Dad would have Christmas Eve with me and Christmas Day with them. He would have Thanksgiving with me and Easter with them. I could never have imagined that the beautiful little girl I loved so dearly would be gone from my life, and like the split with Mary Anne, it broke my heart.

The Lonely Boy

Chapter 9   A New Focus for Richard

Now that pretty much all my family ties had been severed, I began to focus on my career. I was very successful at my job in sales and I'd become the most successful salesman in my division in company history. I was promoted to our new Internet division and I was able to work from home since I had a west coast territory.

I got Gerard my old job and we started working together. Gerard had become my best friend and was now more like a brother to me. When family events would come up and he found out I wasn't included, he would go out of his way to do nice things for me and I always appreciated the love and attention. I was also doing very well at my design business, which I named Mavin Hill Designs. I was making more money than I ever had before. It was my first real taste of success.

I went out and bought myself a silver Mercedes. We put in a pool and finished the basement. We redid the kitchen and installed Viking appliances and granite countertops, and we redecorated the interior of the house. We also started taking elaborate trips again and having grand parties. Each time we had a party I always invited my sisters. They never once even responded. I think our success made them like us even less. I think they felt like I was bragging or showing off. They never realized that I just wanted them in my life.

The Lonely Boy

Our newfound success also became an issue with some of our friends. Someone once told me that as you become more successful, your friends will change. They said they will begin to resent you and they'll find ways to pull away. When they look at you now, they see their own failures and shortcomings. Over time, I began to feel that with some of our friends, this was becoming true. But I had always liked having people around me and we had a lot of friends. As time went on, my friends became my family. The family I was born to gravitated around my sisters and no one even called except my father who was a constant in my life.

John had still not come out to his family. His parents were older and very conservative. He kept that part of his life separate. They knew we lived together, but nothing was ever discussed. I think it was hard for John. John had a brother who died at 18 of leukemia. Vincent was the straight brother who would have given his parents grandchildren. John had difficulty with survivor's guilt, feeling he should have been the one to go. He loved his family, but kept them separate from his life with me. As I began to grow older, I realized that this was going to be another hurdle in my life. John was very torn. He was proud of his life and what we were building together, but he felt his parents would never understand. John's parents spent winters in Florida and Myrtle Beach and he would go four months without seeing them. One year, when they returned, he decided to invite them for the weekend. He slept in the spare room. His dad was nice to me, but his mother didn't warm up to me at all. She didn't understand the dynamic of our relationship and it was awkward for both of us. I must say I was very disappointed in John at this time. We had now been together for seven years and it was time for him to make peace with himself and for all of us to get to the next level.

The weekend that John's parents came to stay with us required much planning. There was shopping and cleaning and all sorts of things to get the house perfect. We had just done the kitchen over and finished the basement. We wanted everything to be perfect. One thing I can say about our relationship is that we always work well together when it comes to entertaining. John was a Culinary Institute graduate and he had owned a catering company. The food was always perfect. He could make it look effortless and flawless at the same time. I had the design business now, so the backdrop was always very beautiful. This was a mixed blessing for us. It made our good friends feel proud and honored to be there, but it intimidated others. Over time it became more of a problem. Some people thought we were bragging, not just wanting things to be special for our guests. I began to see the difference between the two and started to realize who our true friends were and who we needed to move away from. Having a mother that basically walked away from me eight years before she died and a father that was not much of a father, I clung to my

The Lonely Boy

friendships for love and support. When I became aware that someone did not have our best interests at heart, I took it very hard.

People who I loved began to get very jealous of John and I as money came in.   Little things would lead to big things, and ultimately, to a parting of ways. I hated to lose anyone from my life. It's the one thing that always sends me into depression. I have battled depression on and off for years but I was always able to bounce back from it. In the years that followed, the depression grew deeper and it became harder and harder to overcome. Also, like everything in life, things continue to change and when our luck began to change, some of the people we loved so dearly cut their ties with us.

That is why I try so hard in life. I value love and friendship most of all. I am a true Taurus. I am loyal to the core, but people change and go away. You will eventually have to accept these changes as a part of life. For me, this was the thing I had the most trouble with. When you get Richard Scuderi as a friend, you get a lifelong commitment. I don't walk away from people. Most people are just not that invested and they don't feel things as deeply as I do.

This is where the lonely boy comes in. I have always had the ability to see the value of love and friendship, even when I was surrounded by people that didn't have the same capacity to accept it and love back. For most of my life, I had to struggle. I was the gay kid on the school bus. I was

The Lonely Boy

the victim of sexual molestation at puberty. I had parents that were very unhappy with each other and with me. There was so much bad in my life, all I wanted to do was find peace. I went to extraordinary means to do that all in the name of love and kindness. It was often mistaken for a sense of superiority and thus it accomplished just the opposite. It alienated people and took them from me. It was a balance I wouldn't get right until many years later in my life.

John's mother was very difficult and cold at this point in our relationship. She would come to dinner with her daughters and the three of them would only talk to each other. They wouldn't even acknowledge me. They would push their dirty dishes towards me to clean up when they were done eating. It was very disappointing. There were several incidents that caused a great deal of grief with his family. The first was when John turned 40. His sister hosted a 40th birthday party for him and didn't invite me, even though we were living together. I had to have my own separate party for John with our friends. The second incident was when we first built our house. When she first visited, John's other sister looked around our house and told me that there were plenty of things in my house that were her family heirlooms and that they belonged to her. She told me that if something happened to John she was going to come in and take them from me. She said they belonged to her children, not to me. This was awful. His

The Lonely Boy

married sister was jealous and it showed. There were many incidents such as these. I always turned the other cheek and moved on, but it added to my depression and overall unhappiness.

John's mother had a habit of showing up with a house gift that was something John and I would never want and that was not to our taste. We had a shelf full of Leahy garage sale items in our linen closet. One weekend his mother brought us a black plant stand. It didn't go with our décor nor go with anything we had, but we graciously accepted it and I put it out immediately, as I did all of her gifts when they would visit.

This particular visit would prove to be extremely lethal. They stayed for three days, a little too long. I decided I would kill her with kindness this time and win her over. She loved interior design and told me she went to school for it. I was in the early years of my business. I was only doing it part time since I still worked in corporate America during the week but I decided I would to take her to a high end design store on Saturday and get her my discount.

We went out and shopped all afternoon. She commented on how lovely everything was. But when we came home she called one of her daughters on my phone and I overheard her saying I took her to junk stores. She bought a bottle of bright red nail polish when we were out and she decided to polish her nails in my new pale blue and white guest suite with white rugs. She had no respect for my home or for me. Then, when they came down for Saturday night dinner, she looked me up and down and said, "Is that what you're wearing?" I wanted this woman out of my house. On Sunday morning John took his parents to church. His mother asked me not to join them since she wanted alone time with him.

In the years that followed however, I came to really love John's mother. It was hard for me to even write this part of the book, but it proves that life does change and people can change at any age if they open their hearts. I never commented on their behavior and I never confronted them, but it really bothered me. We tried to keep their visits to a minimum, but his mother would always want to visit. I never understood why. If she was uncomfortable with our relationship, I couldn't understand why she didn't just stay home or meet John out. Don't come to my home and be disrespectful.

On the work front, things were thriving. We were in the thick of the dot com years, and I was in the right place at the right time. I had gotten a promotion to the company's new Internet division and I really started to get noticed. This, however, was a conservative company that wasn't at all gay friendly. I knew I needed to keep my personal life separate, but as time went on it became harder and harder to do that. I won a great deal of awards and with them came company trips to resorts in Florida, Arizona, California, and Mexico. I always went alone. On one trip to Disney

The Lonely Boy

years earlier, I took my sister Jennifer. I always felt my personal life needed to be kept private.

I was pretty content at this point in my life. John and I were getting along, my career was doing well and I was well liked at work. My design business was also taking off. I was working in mansions and being well received. I began to realize that work brought me the most joy now. I hired my dad to work with me on some of my design projects and that brought us closer together. Work became the focus of my life now and it was very fulfilling. I hadn't lost hope of reuniting my family, but the success I experienced at work and in our social life made me quite content and the days seemed to pass quite quickly.

Our closest friends were the couple we met when we were all living in the planned community called The Hills in Bedminster, New Jersey. Marie and Ross were a little older than us but we found we had a great deal in common. We all came from dysfunctional families so we were even spending our holidays together now. Ross had a successful flooring business and Marie owned a very successful relocation business. Marie started out in Alphabet City in a small one bedroom flat with her mother and two brothers. I think she and her mother even had to share a bed. She came from very modest means, but was ambitious and very bright. She became a realtor after her first marriage ended and she really found her calling. She was charming and a natural salesperson. She quickly became a broker and then

The Lonely Boy

opened up a relocation company. Like me, she wasn't appreciated for how special she was, but she always strived to be the best at everything she did. She eventually became very successful and shared with us the fruits of her labor. She joined the posh Fiddler's Elbow Country Club. We spent our weekends having dinner in the wine cellar and enjoying private 4th of July fireworks at the club. They bought a beautiful new home and built a brand new second residence in Florida. Marie and Ross really encouraged us in our relationship and when opportunities came up they were the first to help.

It was 2001 when we hosted the first of what would come to be many Labor Day parties. We invited Marie and Ross, Gerard, my dad and his girlfriend of the moment, and a couple across the street we had become close to, Bob and Jenny. Our group was changing but this was the core. We had just finished our deck that September and we had the party out on the deck under a small canvas canopy I had just added. I waited a long time for a really nice deck and was out there every day trying to make it even better.

Early September had been particularly beautiful that year and I was working at home now on a laptop. Sometimes I would host webinars with my west coast clients live from my deck. On the morning of September 11th, I was on the phone early in the morning with my friend Peter. We had met years earlier at one of the GAAMC meetings. We were talking when all of a sudden he just stopped.

The Lonely Boy

"What's wrong?" I asked.

"I see burning papers outside my window," he said.

"What are you talking about?" I responded.

"I have to go," he said. "I'll call you back."

I didn't think much of it and went inside to get a cup of coffee. The Today Show was on. All of a sudden, they broke to a news story about something happening at the World Trade Center where Peter had just started a new job. When I saw the massive hole in the first tower, I knew that a tragedy was unfolding. I dialed frantically but got no answer and no voice mail. I kept dialing and dialing. As the events unfolded, I called John and asked him to come home but he was told to stay where he was.

My dad called right after the Pentagon was hit. I lost some TV reception and my cell phone stopped working. I was in a panic and my dad stayed on the landline with me for a very long time. I will never forget that day. We stayed on the phone and shared the moments together. It would be hours before John came home. Bob and Jenny came over that evening and together we watched the TV coverage in horror. I was afraid that my friend was dead, but late in the day I got a call from him from a payphone near the Brooklyn Bridge. He told me that after he hung up with me he got up to see what was going on. His tower had not been hit yet. When he got to the Sky Lobby to change elevators, an announcement came over the public address system telling staff to remain in the building because there was

The Lonely Boy

debris falling from the first tower hit. They were advised to return to their desks. Peter's boss said, "Nothing is ever going to happen to this building." His colleagues went back to their desks but Peter got scared and left. The rest is history. Everyone he worked with was killed.

I was so happy he was ok, but when I went to see him a few days later, I could tell he was really shaken up. It took him a long time for him to feel safe again. My boss told me to cancel all my appointments. I didn't go back to work for another week. We all just watched television as the world came to a halt. No planes in the air, no travel into New York City, and fear in everyone's eyes. It was such a sudden and sharp contrast to September 10th, only a day before. As I always said, life is temporary and unpredictable. You have to savor the good moments because that will not last.

Work became my happy place and really fulfilled me. I won so many awards at my job I began to get teased that I had naked pictures of someone around. But not everybody was happy for me. My friend Gerard was becoming snarky with me and he got very friendly with our group Admin. He wasn't even waiting for me anymore when I came in for meetings. He was struggling in my old job and resented me for doing so well.

The apex of my work success came shortly after when I was named salesperson of the year at my company. I made

The Lonely Boy

my entire sales quota for the year by May 1st. No one in the history of the company had ever achieved that before. I had traveled all over the world for this job and it was the second happiest period of my life. Up 'til that point, I had always gone on my awards trips alone, but this time I had won a week in Hawaii with all the bells and whistles. I didn't want John to miss it. This would also be the first time I was flying after 9/11, and I wasn't getting on a plane without him. We thought about it long and hard and I decided I just had to bring him. We'd have a fabulous time. Times had changed and we decided we may have been paranoid all those years. I used to be the only one at work functions without a spouse. I was sure they figured out that I wasn't alone at 37 years old.

John and I both had a lot of vacation time and we decided to make it a three week trip. We'd spend a week in San Francisco, a week in Hawaii for the work trip, and then a week in Napa Valley and Sonoma. We were doing well, but this trip was a little decadent even for us. Our week in San Francisco was amazing. It's a great food city and we enjoyed learning about the different neighborhoods and cultures. When we were in Nob Hill, we decided to stop for a drink at the famous Fairmont Hotel. While we were walking through the hotel lobby I had a chance encounter with Matthew Shepard's mother. Our eyes connected for only a few seconds, but when I looked into her eyes, I saw incredible pain. It all happened in a flash and I said to John,

The Lonely Boy

"Did you see who that was?" He said, "It was the mother." I just wanted to tell her that her son's life was important to us. I just wanted to hug this woman. I felt her pain. But there was a large wedding reception going on. She disappeared into a big crowd, and we lost her. I hope someday I'll have the chance to tell her how much her son's life meant to the world and how special and important he was.

We departed San Francisco and went on to our week in Hawaii. My company put us up in a beautiful resort in Maui and I got to meet a lot of new people from corporate that I never met before. On the night of the awards banquet, I was seated at the President's Table. This was a great honor since there were hundreds of people in the room from all over the world.

John and I could tell at once that we were not well received. No one was talking to us and it became uncomfortable by the end of the night. I received my award on stage and had my picture taken. It was also recorded on video. That night we started having a bad feeling about the whole thing. There was a breakfast meeting the next day which featured a video of the week in review. John and I were edited out of it. Something was very wrong. We left after breakfast thinking we made a mistake, but there was nothing we could do about it now.

When we landed back in California we had a near miss with another plane. It was quite scary for a minute or so. I began to feel my luck was beginning to change for the worse.

The Napa Valley part of the trip was fantastic. John surprised me and rented a navy blue Jaguar convertible which barely fit our three weeks' worth of luggage. We did wonderful things like dine in the first class all glass car on the wine train and eat at five star restaurants. Still, I was concerned about what I had just done. I often thought that what had happened with my family made me seem a little too sensitive, so I told myself I shouldn't be so paranoid. After all, I was making these people money. Surely that was all that corporate cared about. But when I went back to work, I learned that I was losing my lucrative west coast territory and was being shifted to a less lucrative one with the same quota. Now I became quite concerned. They brought in a new boss. He had been at the President's Table that night and had dinner with John and me. His wife actually sat next to me and never spoke to me once. The first thing this new boss did was sit down privately with each of the salespeople on his team. I was concerned about my turn but it never came. He never even sat down with me. Gerard said I was the only one who didn't have a one to one interview. He told me the new boss asked a lot of personal questions and wanted to know about interests and family life. He said he felt like he'd been profiled. I was very concerned so I called my direct supervisor. He told me

The Lonely Boy

I should keep my options open and start looking for another job. "Read between the lines," he said.

I was in a panic. John did some research and found a lawyer through an LGBT organization. She met with me and told me to keep a journal and to buy a tape recorder. I did just that. I was still doing very well but I started interviewing with other companies just in case.

On a Friday afternoon two weeks before Christmas in 2002, I received a FedEx package with a plane ticket to the Bahamas. I made President's Circle again. Three hours later that same day, I received work force reduction papers. What was even worse was that my friend Gerard, me, and another gay employee were the only ones let go. The other two had been offered a severance package that day which they signed for. I had them meet with my attorney on Monday. She told them they had a three day right to rescind and they did. We then sued the company for discrimination.

I was devastated. My identity hinged on being successful at my job. For fear that I would be seen as a failure, I accepted another offer and was at an inside sales job with my company's biggest competitor by the second week in January. It was a much lower level job and it paid a lot less money. It was a big step down for me. I had to work in a gray cubical and be in the office by 7 am. I didn't tell anyone, including my father. I was so upset. I felt rejected and ashamed at the same time. In retrospect, I shouldn't have gone back to work so soon. The other two men let go didn't work again for several years. I had pride and I didn't want anyone to see a gap in my employment. In addition to that, our expenses were high now and I couldn't afford to stay home. I worked with nice people who took me right in, but I started having emotional problems. After several months, I became depressed again and started having panic attacks. One day I broke down in the stairwell and started crying. I just couldn't do it. I quit and went home with no job in sight.

This was a one of the lowest points in my life. I felt completely deflated and wasn't sure if I ever wanted to work for anyone else again. John suggested I focus full time on my design business. He wasn't worried about the money. He said I was very talented and the money would come. Even so, I was very shaken and no longer confident in my abilities. As I always said, savor the good moments. Things will never stay the same for long.

The Lonely Boy

CHAPTER 10 New Beginnings and Sad Endings

In the spring of 2003, a chance meeting with an old friend brought a new opportunity. Jay, a friend of mine, had just broken up with his partner of 30 years. They owned a very successful business, a large boutique. Half was devoted to a women's clothing boutique and the rest was an interior design studio. My friend offered me the chance to take over the design studio as my own and do it full time.

John really encouraged me and I decided to do it. We stripped the space to the wallboard and I put my mark on it. We painted a rich new color on the walls and I brought in all new inventories. I was very worried about not having a salary, so I went to the paint store myself to ask if they'd give me a trade discount. After a quick conversion with the paint shop manager I was on my way. Later that day, I received my first call on my new store phone. The guy from the paint store, Victor, had referred me to a wealthy couple in Harding and on the first day I opened they booked a $35,000 renovation job with me. It was like a sign from God. This was what I was meant to do with my life! From the moment I opened, the business was a raging success. I hired a new accountant and asked her if she thought I was doing ok? She said she had never seen this kind of first quarter in a brand new business. I was very encouraged and the work kept coming in.

The Lonely Boy

I became very worried about Gerard though. He took the firing very hard and still wasn't even looking for a job. I brought him in to work for me and he did small projects from time to time. He had great taste and loved to shop with me for the store. I told him he should do it too, but he didn't have the ambition or confidence to do it himself. His parents had really hurt him and I saw a guy with great potential not using his gifts because of the grief that others put on him. I feel like being a gay man is a curse. At least it was for me. You're always looking over your shoulder. I have gotten really good at changing pronouns and keeping my life a secret. My life is as important as anyone else's and I resent all the grief we face for something that isn't our fault. It is just a realization.

We went to court for a pretrial hearing and our attorney assured us we had a great case. The company let me go when I was at 235% of quota. That was going to hurt them. But Gerard was a mess. At the time he was let go, he was only at 80% of quota and was put on a plan, as was Tony, the other gay employee. If I wasn't there, they wouldn't have had a case. Tony and Gerard worked in the office. I was in the Internet division and worked virtually so I didn't know Tony that well. John and I hosted a Christmas party that year and invited Tony and his boyfriend as well as Gerard. Weeks later, Tony had a dinner and only included Gerard. I was surprised and hurt by that. I wondered what was going on.

The Lonely Boy

In the meantime, I had gotten a call from my old boss. I taped the call, and he incriminated himself. Our attorney told the other two plaintiffs to buy tape recorders so if they got calls we could gather more evidence. They did.

I tried not to let things get me down and I focused on my new career. I was 38 years old now and in a better place in my life, but I must admit I still thought about Brian from time to time. The love I had with him was so powerful; I had never felt anything like it before or since. I always regretted that we never saw it to completion. It was taken from me at the same time my mother was. It was 17 years later, and I must admit that even though I loved John, I was still a little in love with Brian. I always felt that I left a part of myself with him and at times I didn't think I was giving John as much of myself as I could give him. We had a great life, but I never had the same chemistry with John as I'd had with Brian. Of course, we were older now and when you're with someone for a long time, things change. But there was a sadness in my heart that never went away. Christmas came quickly that year. I got home early on Christmas Eve and realized I'd lost John's card. I had settled in for the night, planning only to wrap presents, so I was in sweats and sneakers. An inner voice told me to get changed before I went out to buy a new card and I did.

While I was picking out cards, I felt someone looking at me through the front window. It was Brian. I could always feel his presence. He came into the store and I was happy to see him. We spoke a few words and we wished each other a Merry Christmas. He told me he was single now and looking for a last minute gift for his nephew who was all grown up.

Karma is so twisted. The year after we broke up, I saw him in a card store through a window right before Christmas. That time he did not see me. He had gained a great deal of weight after we broke up and I wasn't really sure it was him at first but then I saw the white Corvette out front. I could see through that window he was buying a Christmas love card for someone. I went home and cried all night. This time, 17 years later, it was he who was looking at me buying the love card. I had the relationship and he was alone now. I am so glad something told me to change and get dressed. When I got home I told John what had happened he said, "You're still in love with him aren't you?" I said no, but he could see it in my eyes. This man was so cruel to me. How could I still have feelings for him?

The spring of 2004 came and I was busier than ever. I couldn't answer the calls fast enough and I didn't have enough contractors for all the jobs I was bidding on. I was really in the right place at the right time again. I would work in mansions and then come back to my modest four bedroom colonial. I decided to bring in an architect to add some dormers and a sunroom. If I was going to entertain for work at my house, the house had to be a lot more impressive. After meetings with an architect and a few different contractors we were all in agreement that it would be difficult to grow the house. The house we built had a steep lot and issues with setbacks. They all advised me to look for a bigger house in the same neighborhood.

John had great instincts and found an amazing house not far away. It was way too expensive for us, but it had been sitting on the market for a long time. It had fallen into foreclosure because of a bad divorce and by now had been sitting empty for three years. John said, "Let's make a low bid on it." He said, "When the bank is paying to heat that big house with its three furnaces, they'll take our offer." So we put in a low bid, but it was rejected.

I still couldn't get Brian out of my head and one night after too many glasses of wine the subject came up again. John said, "You will never have peace until you finish it with Brian." He said, "I think if you saw him again, the spell you felt might be broken. You are confusing your feelings about your mother's death with feelings for him. He is your connection to the past and that's why it is so strong for you."

He told me he trusted me and knew I would do the right thing.

After three weeks of thinking about it, I got up the nerve to call Brian. I prayed that his machine would come on so I could just leave a message. That way, if he didn't want to talk to me, he just wouldn't call back. I thought back to the call I made in 1988 when he told me he'd met someone else

The Lonely Boy

and not to call again. I wasn't sure if I could handle that. I left a quick message, and several hours later he actually called back. I was so excited. I told him I opened had a shop in Bernardsville and that he should come by sometime. He said, "Great, then I can take you to lunch."

We set a date and I booked a table at a beautiful French restaurant near my store. "I'm 17 years older now," I thought, "So I better look good." I worked out every day. I bought the best outfit I could find and tried to look young. In truth, at 38, I probably looked better than I had ever looked in my life.

The day finally came. I waited and waited and he never showed. Hours later, I got a message that he couldn't make it and he wanted to reschedule. I was crushed. He called that night and apologized profusely. We rescheduled and I told him to make the plans this time. I wasn't going to put a lot of effort into it.

We met in New Brunswick at a Mexican restaurant that we used to go to often. It was still very 1980s and it hadn't changed a bit. When we saw each other, the sparks flew. There was still chemistry on both our parts, but I felt like I was having lunch with an old friend. Our lunch lasted three hours and when I went to use the rest room, a man struck up a conversation. It was obvious that he was flirting. Brian noticed it when I came back to the table and he commented on it. I was feeling pretty good now. He took me out for dessert afterwards, and just as we always did back in the day, we shared our dessert—one dessert with two spoons.

He looked different. He was older now and not as stunning as he was in 1986, but I was still attracted to him and I could tell that he was still attracted to me too. When he told me he was working as a handyman, I was kind of disappointed. He had had great dreams when we were both young. Seventeen years later, he was still living in the same apartment and he was driving a rundown old Suburban.

After our lunch, I decided that I would keep Brian in my life, but at a safe distance. It would help my healing process and improve my relationship with John, I thought. It's much more powerful to love a ghost than a real person. John knew this guy was terrible to me. The core of someone doesn't change, and when I saw Brian again I would realize he was not a good guy.

Work was hectic and I was installing 13 blinds for a commercial job. The installer never showed and I needed help. I remembered that Brian used to install blinds when he was younger. I called to ask if would he help me and he said he would. I paid him and I took him to lunch afterwards. We talked for three hours.

I couldn't deny it. I was still in love with the guy and I was convinced he was still in love with me. I began hiring him for more of my business projects. It was an excuse to spend more time with him, and every time it led to a great meal and hours of conversation.

The Lonely Boy

One week when John was away at a conference, Brian invited me over for dinner. I was scared, and I wondered if I should go? I thought about it for days, but I was very curious, so I went.

I turned into that familiar street and I was still in awe of how beautiful it was. As I drove down the long driveway to his garage apartment, I noticed that the white Corvette he bought so many years back was now disabled and under a tarp. At some point, he had painted the front door red and it did not look good.

When I went inside, I could tell that nothing much had changed. But it just looked so run down now. The toilets were dark brown and the appliances were really old. But I was just so happy to be there, I put those thoughts aside.

Brian made us London broil and shrimp for dinner and it was really good. I specifically remember thinking, "I'm back!!!"

I suggested that we eat in the living room on the large coffee table just like we used to. At one point he looked into my eyes and told me he loved me and we spent the night together. The next morning I was in his arms again and I was in heaven. I must say that at the time I didn't see this coming, but in retrospect it was inevitable. I have only had sex with two men in my life, Brian and John. I had fooled around with a few people in my single years but I have little sexual experience. My molestation made me fearful of sex, and after the onset of AIDS, it wasn't worth taking any chances. The walk of shame to get blood work and the two-week waiting period put that in perspective real fast.

Brian and I continued to work together and that's when and where I saw him socially. We always spent time together after work and I loved it. I began to notice however that there were inconsistencies in his life. He didn't have a bank account. When I gave him a check, he would have to go back to the bank and cash it. He didn't have a cell phone. You couldn't get in touch with him until he called you. In addition, he seemed to be very much of a loner, one who was primarily interested in very young men. At one point, he had mentioned that his town had a big Hispanic population and he told me he loved looking at the very young Spanish boys. Then I had a flash. Several years earlier, I saw a report on the news that the authorities were looking for a dark suburban. Some man was talking to a 14 year old Hispanic boy on a bicycle trying to get him to come home with him. I began to wonder if that man was Brian. I also learned that his parents weren't talking to him. I wondered if was that why? He hadn't moved from the same apartment in the past 17 years. He barely worked and he had no health insurance. Why did an adult man have to cash checks on the spot? Had he been arrested? Did he have a criminal record? I also noticed that I was always giving and he was always taking. On the night of his birthday, I was cuddling with him all evening. He suddenly got up and decided that he wanted to go to a gay bar. I went home. My life had become sophisticated and great. His ex-boyfriend, the one after me, walked away from him. Maybe it was Brian who had the problem.

The next time I saw Brian, he bragged that he had hooked up with a very good-looking young guy on the night of his birthday.

What had I done? This guy was a loser and he was never going to be good to me or anyone. That's who he was. He just liked to play.

One day after a job, we went out for Thai food. I told him I was upset he was with someone else. He said he was sorry. He didn't mean to hurt me. He said he cared for me as much as anyone else he had ever been with.

I never slept with him again.

After that, I went in for a blood test. Although we did very little during our time together and it was safe, I needed confirmation. I found out I was fine. I went in for tests for the next year and a half and I was always ok. Sex isn't worth it.

Brian continued to work for me on occasion, but now just as friends. One night I was at his apartment and I looked into his eyes. I remember the first time I looked into his eyes. I saw the most beautiful blue eyes with the longest dark eyelashes. I looked into his eyes and I saw love. That's the reason why I chose him to be the first man I was ever with. Now, as a test, when I looked into his eyes and all I saw were snake eyes, cold with no love. He was still very handsome, but the love I thought I saw in him was gone. I stopped seeing him socially and started to look for another handyman.

When I called him in a pinch a few weeks later to give him some work he said, "What's in it for me?"

I was done and now so regretful and wracked with guilt. I am not a cheater by nature. What had I done? I confessed to John and I hurt him with that. I should have kept it to myself. We got beyond it, and I give him credit for that. I'm not sure that if things had been reversed that I would forgive him or continue our relationship.

I went back to focusing on my business. I was also becoming concerned about our dog Cajun, who was 13 years old now and having trouble walking. We took him to the vet and he told us Cajun was riddled with cancer. They told us to put him down, but we couldn't. We kept him going through incontinence and lethargy. In the end, we had to feed him boiled rice and hose him off after he relieved himself because his legs finally gave out. When we brought him to the vet to put him down we had to carry him in on a board. I wasn't sure it was time, but the doctor said it was. They gave him the first shot and he grew sleepy. We fed him treats and for the first time in weeks he ate them heartily. I said, "Stop, he's responding!" Our vet said, "That happens at the end."

The Lonely Boy

Cajun began to snore and John said, "Let's go." He was very emotional and he left the room. I stayed with Cajun and held him until he crossed over. It was devastating. I have never I had a dog since because I loved him that much. I felt even worse for John. Cajun was his dog. I came in after the fact.

Our vet came back into the room told us they would cremate Cajun and send us his ashes. I screamed "No!" and asked for other options. She told us there was a pet cemetery in northwest New Jersey called Abbey Glen. "It's a lot more expensive option," she said. I begged John to do it. We drove up to make the arrangements and the depression we felt on the way up was overwhelming.

But we did it. Cajun had a casket and a viewing.

Coincidentally, Cajun was buried next to our friend Jay's dog. We only found out when we saw the headstone next to Cajun's plot. Jay is the one from the shop where I started my design business. When we saw Cajun during the viewing we knew we did right by him and we both spontaneously felt better.

Soon after, the company that had let me go made a settlement and I came into a large sum of money. On a cold snowy day in February, just as John predicted, the bank accepted our offer on the new house and because I had a nest egg from the trial, we were able to buy it without selling our current one. Once again, the timing was perfect. It was as if someone was watching over us. We were doing

The Lonely Boy

it. We were moving on up. I hated the house now without Cajun in it. This would be a brand new start for both of us.

2005 was the year I was turning 40 and we wanted to celebrate it in a big way. Business was good and I was working on the new house while we were trying to sell the one we built. Through Marie we were able to book the posh Fiddler's Elbow Country Club for my birthday and we were planning a party complete with a sit down dinner and dancing. Frank from high school had come back into my life yet again and was staying over on weekends. Frank told us we should stay where we were and I began to see the repeat pattern of him bailing or doing something bad when something good would happen to me. He turned 40 before I did, in February. We took him to the Chart House with a new guy he just met. The guy was really unsophisticated and wrong for him. When Frank went to the bathroom, the guy asked us if Frank was a good guy or a bad one. It made us feel bad. We really tried to make him feel special that night because he wasn't in a good place in his life. The next day, instead of thanking me, he told me I looked like I wasn't feeling well and said I looked awful. The likely reason was that I told him to dress for dinner the night and while John and I showed up in jackets, he and his young friend wore jeans and sweaters. Frank had put on weight and his was a little too tight. I think he felt insecure. I let it go, but when he realized we were buying a very large home, he began to get snarky with me. One night when he stayed over I saw him peck John good night and then go in for a second kiss. I watched but did not try to intervene. The next night I confronted John. He said it was innocent, but this was a pattern with Frank. He tried to sleep with me and ruined my relationship with Paula. He slept with my girlfriend Wendy after we broke up when I was still questioning my sexuality. When I bought my first condo, he didn't talk to me for six months because he said he hated it. I want longstanding friendships so much that I have a high tolerance for pain, but this was obviously a bad guy.

When my birthday came Frank didn't show and I never saw him again. The party went on and it was lovely, but not without a few crises. All the friends came but my sisters did not. Uncle Jack and Aunt Maria told John he was inconveniencing them by planning a Friday night party. Uncle Jack never showed. Aunt Maria said she had to think about it. When she learned that many of the other relatives were coming, she waited to RSVP until the night before the party and arrived with one of them. She came without her husband or daughter and her gift to me was a gift certificate from Tiffany's in the exact amount of the value of the locket with my mother's picture in it I had given her daughter. I knew it was to show me she returned the locket. The card attached said, "Happy Birthday from Uncle Jack and Aunt Maria." I just don't get the message, do I?

The Lonely Boy

Then tragedy struck. Three days before the party, John's father died. Now we were in trouble. The country club wouldn't let John cancel and his family was putting pressure on him not to go. John's father had been a funeral director and the family was having two funerals back to back. The first would be in Queens, where they grew up, and the second in Westchester, where they had retired. It went on for four whole days. John stayed with his family, and Gerard drove with me to Queens for moral support. The next day, John went to the second day of the wake but skipped the evening session so he could be with me at my party. That's the thing about life; you never know what lies around the corner. His family didn't want him to go and they gave him grief for being there for me. In addition, my dad had a bad case of gout that night and barely danced. But all in all, I had a great time and I am grateful for having such a caring man to love me.

A week later, on my actual 40th birthday we went for our lungs and bought the big house. We took on a $1.3 million dollar bridge loan and it was scary and exciting at the same time. It took a long time to repair the house with the water damage and all the work we wanted to do. By the end of September we were finally done. I purposely set the moving day for September 28th, which was Mary Anne's birthday. I wanted that day to become a new good memory for us. So in 2005, we closed on my birthday, April 21, and moved in on hers, September 28, so we'd be in, in time for the holidays. We were excited to have Thanksgiving in that big new dining room and to use all the fireplaces. It was the new start we both needed.

One of the most interesting gifts I received from my party was from a friend named Deborah. She is a very spiritual person, and she gave me a psychic reading from a friend of hers. The friend had seen me out one day and she told Deborah she had a great deal to tell me. I didn't even know the reading was going to happen. I was at Deborah's house for something and she said, "This is for you." When I turned around, a beautiful blonde woman was standing there. She told me to sit and we would speak. I only had one psychic reading before, on the Valentine's Day after Brian dumped me. That lady told me I would meet a man with the first initial J and we would be together for a long time. She was right on the money with that. I kept an open mind and just listened to what this lady had to say. The first question she asked was, "Who is Jennifer? Your mother is so mad at her," she said. I was amazed. I was so hurt by my sister Jennifer walking away from me. How could she know that? She said I didn't have good people around me and told me there were a lot of people who were jealous because I had white light around me. She said my word was truth and if I said something I would follow through with it. She told me she saw me driving a new sports car soon, something sharp and snazzy. She then told me something I was not prepared to hear. She told me that I have lived on earth many times before and I was a very old soul. She said in my last life I was a very beautiful woman. I was so beautiful that I took advantage of people and didn't care about them. My last life ended early at the hands of someone else. My karma in life this time was to come back with incredible sensitivity and compassion and be surrounded by people who wouldn't appreciate it and would never understand me. If I did a good job at this, at mid life there would be a cosmic change and the balance of my life would be very charmed. This time, however, I would use my blessings in a positive way to help others and to do good things with my newfound fortune. Her words rocked me to the core. I didn't believe them or understand them at first. I just thanked her and left.

In the weeks that passed, I started to think that maybe there was some truth in what she said. How did she know about Jennifer? I never told her anything about that. How did she know my mother had passed on? After that I began to explore my spiritual side and went to see this woman often for guidance in my life. The messages were never as direct as that first one though and I found myself trying to push something through that probably needed to unfold as God planned, not as I would prefer. She did however say in a subsequent reading that my father's health would fail and to stay close to him. She also told me I had many people who loved me, especially women, but that my sisters would never be in my life again.

The Lonely Boy

John and I had Thanksgiving that year together with my dad, Marie and Ross—our newly-reinvented makeshift family. My dad began to get close to Marie and Ross and often went to their house. We were worried about Ross at Thanksgiving. His color did not look good and he seemed drawn. Over Christmas, we caught Ross smoking again and read him the riot act. The doctors said if he didn't change his ways, he would need a heart transplant.

Work was very busy and Ross had a carpet and flooring business. I was using him on all my jobs, and began to see a difference in him and his stamina. On New Year's Eve, we hosted a private party at a new restaurant near our home. Ross ate and drank too much that night and two days later he was back in the hospital. Marie also was starting to fail. Her driving was terrible. She had three small accidents in a six month period. She was also becoming a little disoriented and forgetful. We wrote it off to stress but she kept getting worse. When we went to see Ross in the hospital, we were shocked to see that he had been moved to cardiac intensive care. He spent his 65th birthday, March 12, 2006, in the hospital. They were monitoring him closely. He was his ornery self though so we felt hopeful.

By our second visit he was quite different. He was very angry and he asked me to take away the steak that Marie had grilled from home. He had just gotten a new black Mercedes sports coupe, and he pulled the keys out of the drawer and asked Marie to hand them to me. He told me he wanted me to take it and use it. He said it wasn't good for the car to sit unused for too long. I feared he was making his last wishes known. He also gave away his old Porsche to a friend of the family that night. After we left him we went down to the lobby and sat for a while. It was clear to us that he was preparing to die.

A few days later, John called to break the news that Ross was gone. I left the job I was working on and rushed to the hospital. They allowed us to see him in bed. It was the first time I was with someone in the hospital after they had passed. It was very sad. I knew it was coming, but I always thought he would pull through.

Marie seemed to have made peace with it, but we thought she was still in shock. We followed her back to her house in our own cars and at one point she almost had a massive collision. For the next couple of days, we did all the driving. I stopped and got sandwiches and we started making funeral plans. I called my dad from Marie's house and he actually cried on the phone with me. Ross and Marie had become part of his family too.

Marie had an adult daughter from a previous marriage, Gina. She was living in Brooklyn. We waited for her to arrive and started making plans. Ross, like my mom, had a list of instructions and Marie was going to honor them all. He wanted to be laid out at Hillsborough Funeral Home which was near his store. We contacted them and they went and picked him up. The next day we went to the funeral home. There was a service going on and Marie's cell phone starting ringing loudly. Her ringtone was "Livin' La Vida Loca." She couldn't find it in her purse and this went on for a few minutes. It was upsetting at the time but we laugh about it today.

I picked out clothes for Ross and instructed the funeral director to change the lining of his mahogany casket from off white to pale blue. Marie spared no expense. It was classy and perfect. At the repast, everyone got up and told funny stories. Towards the end a little boy told us how nice Ross was to him any we all broke down.

I quickly had to get back to my regular work schedule but Marie would visit often and stay overnight. We would drive her home in the mornings. She was an anxious woman and often by 5:30 am we could hear she was downstairs already, ready to go. One morning after I dropped Marie off it suddenly dawned on me that the psychic said I soon would be driving a snazzy new sports car. I realized that maybe Ross's car was what she was talking about.

With that revelation, I decided to get closer to my father. The psychic also said that dad's health would fail. I even called his doctor to see what was going on, but they wouldn't tell me anything. I encouraged him sell his house and move closer to us. I started meeting him for lunches and stopping for a quick visit at the house when he wasn't working for me. Life is precious and Ross's death hit us all hard. Marie was still pretty independent but she was very lonely. The death of my good friend made me take a long look at my own life. I was still very sad. My sisters were out of my life and longed for more of a connection to family. I realized one day however I still had two wonderful great aunts. They were a big part of my early life and were very kind to me. One was Aunt Grace and the other Aunt Lil. They were my grandmother's sister and sister-in-law.

Aunt Grace was an amazing and beautiful woman. In the early days, she and her husband, my Uncle Guilie, hosted Christmas every year and invited the entire family for an elegant sit down dinner. They also had a summer pool party every Labor Day. There were often 30 or more guests. This lady had class. She would hand write a place card for each guest and set the table with real china and silver for 30. My great uncle was a self-made businessman. He came from modest means but really did something with his life. He was and is an inspiration to me. He became very successful and the two of them became the unofficial patriarch and matriarch of my mother's family.

Aunt Lil was also very beautiful and kind. She and Uncle Vic, who was a great man, moved close to my parents two years before my mother died and we began to see them more often. But after my mother died, it never occurred to me to continue the relationship. After all there was a natural progression to these things. She was gone and they

The Lonely Boy

were my mother's relatives. After mom and grandma were gone I assumed their great love was also over, but then I thought why? I had shied away from extended family because I was gay, but when I'd see them at family funerals they were both particularly nice to me.

When my Uncle Guilie was diagnosed with a brain tumor, I went to see him at home. I brought John with me. Even though Uncle Guilie was ill and couldn't remember who I was he said, "Gracie, get them something to eat." It speaks volumes to how good he was and how they both truly cared about other people. I thought to myself that day, that's what I want to be like. I want to be successful and be able to share my good fortune with my extended family. So what if I was a gay man? John and I were very stable and we had the perfect house for entertaining.

I decided to get closer to both of my aunts and started making little visits. Aunt Lil had recently lost Uncle Vic and after the funeral I reached out to her. I had heard she was having a hard time and wanted to see if I could help. She told me she had to sell the house. She was unhappy about it, but she had no choice now that Uncle Vic was gone. John and I went to see her and my cousin Karen who was living with her. She put out a beautiful spread of food, which was nice but not necessary. She was so warm and kind. It was just what I was missing from my life. I told her I would sell the house for her. "I sold my house in one day without a commission and I will help you," I said. John

155

made me flyers and we put up signs that Sunday morning. I did this for only two Sundays and by the second one we had our buyer. I think Uncle Vic had something to do with making it so easy for us.

Each Sunday, Lil made a beautiful dinner. One Sunday it was lasagna, and the next, the best roast chicken I ever had. I was helping her but it was she who gave me the gift. Her food was her love and I was starved for it. It also made me feel closer to my own mother in a way because I knew I was honoring her memory.

Cousin Karen found them a great apartment and I held a "contents of house" sale for them. When Aunt Lil got settled into the new apartment, I helped settle her estate and had her make a will. She made me the executor and she left her estate to her two daughters. She wanted to leave me money, but I refused.

Much to my surprise, she wanted to date again but she didn't tell me at first. After she was settled, I would just stop by from time to time. On an unplanned visit to her apartment, she opened the door all dressed up, but she was alone. She admitted she was going on her first date after all those years. I was so happy for her. I looked at her as I left and was in awe of how beautiful she was, especially at that moment. She was tiny now and dressed in a beautiful tan suit with a cameo. She had her hair swept up. When I think of her now that's the image that always comes to me, beautiful but strong.

The Lonely Boy

In a quick span of time, I lost them both, but I was glad I had that special time with them. It left me with good memories about my family to draw upon. When bad things happened in the years that followed, I would think of both these wonderful women and smile.

I decided to have a pool party that summer like Aunt Grace always used to do. I invited my extended family and Marie as well. Aunt Grace's son Johnny and I had recently reconnected and I decided to invite him. Johnny and Marie really hit it off that day and much to my surprise went out on a few dates after that. Johnny was about Marie's age. He had been divorced twice and was very bitter about his second wife.

One their first date Marie told him she had MS and she couldn't guarantee she would stay healthy much longer. They went out one or two more times then parted ways. I yelled at her saying, "You didn't need to do that so soon. Let him get to know you first. I think you may have scared him off." Well that was the end of that. I think she knew she was getting worse and was putting plans in place in the event she could no longer take care of herself.

John and I respected her privacy but would do things like check up on the house and keep an eye on her. One October day I had a premonition that something just wasn't right. I came home from work on a Saturday and decided to check on her. The car was in the driveway but she wasn't at home. It hit me then that she must be seeing someone. The next day I went over to the house to confront her. I was right, she had a boyfriend. She said she met him online. His name was Bill. It was very new but she said really liked him.

I left very upset although I didn't let Marie know how I felt. She had given Ross a great life and had honored all his wishes in death, but we weren't ready to have someone to take his place, at least not yet. I told Marie that I was going to give her Ross's car back so she could sell it. She told me to keep it. I said it was too expensive. "Let's work out a deal," she said. In the end, I agreed to redecorate her den and paint the house in lieu of a check for the car.

We went to Motor Vehicles together and put the car in my name. I started working on Marie's house the next day. I had done a lot of work there when Ross was alive. John actually found them the house, so we were really in it with them from the beginning. I even had my dad build them a new custom mantle in their living room. Each time I came in to work, I prepared myself to meet her new beau, but she was keen enough to keep it separate.

After several months she asked Bill to meet us and he agreed. When we got to the house he was there. It felt weird. He looked a lot like Ross. He was tall and thin and had gray hair. It kind of freaked us out. He was a good-looking guy and Marie was looking very happy. I could tell she was in love. I think it was just as awkward for Bill to meet us as it was for us to meet him. Marie began spending a great deal of time with him and we started to see her less and less.

In the fall of 2006, we were all invited to a Halloween party. Ross had a group of friends that kept in contact with Marie even after Ross died. In fact, one of them bought the carpet store from Marie to take it off her hands. These were very nice people and I think they were just as uncomfortable meeting Bill as we were. He looked a lot like Ross and that made us all feel sad. I even think that may have been why we were included on the guest list.

It was a costume party and everyone was dressed.

Bill owned a bunch of cars and that night he was driving an old Brady Bunch station wagon that we made fun of. We called it the "swagon." I think it made him a little mad but he was driving so it meant we could drink. The more the night passed we could see why Marie liked him. He was a really nice guy. We had a lot of fun that night. Ginger, a single older woman in their group didn't understand my dynamic with John and she put the moves on him. It was really fun to watch. She wrote her phone number on a cocktail napkin and left it with him. Marie didn't particularly like Ginger and we dubbed her "the girl with no gaydar." We laughed about it the whole way home.

Marie and Ross used to host a very nice Christmas party every December and Marie wanted to do it again that year. She asked John to help hire a caterer and a bartender and she asked me to decorate the house for Christmas. We did just that. On the afternoon of the party, Bill and Marie had a fight and he went home. I think Marie wanted to have the party to formally introduce Bill to the rest of her friends and family. We weren't very happy with him when he bailed. He did it again a week later when we took her out for her birthday and once again on New Year's Eve.

We had been invited to a neighbor's house party that night. At 4 pm when we found out that she had been stood up on New Years Eve, we picked her up and brought her with us. We were leery of Bill now, but we didn't ever judge. We just didn't want to see her hurt.

She was never one to ever put up with drama but with him see did. It was a new dynamic for her, because she never let Ross get away with anything. It seemed with Bill she was different. She was changing and ready to commit again. We could see he was a good man. They were just going through growing pains in their new relationship.

The Lonely Boy

Chapter 11   The Tribute

In January of 2007, I realized that March 18th would mark the 20th anniversary of my mom's death. I was very unhappy at her funeral mass. The priest didn't have one personal story about her and how special she was. As an adult now, I had been to many funerals and repasts, including Ross's. They were all so special and personal. At a recent service for a man who had been an actor, Kathleen, his wife, rented a theatre in their town and put on a tribute show for her husband. She had the marquee read "David Spellcoleman's It's a Wonderful Life." It was the most touching thing I had ever seen.

I decided that I wanted to have a memorial service and luncheon for my mother. I had the money and the resources and I was going to invite my sisters and see what would happen. My sisters had been out of my life for years now, but I thought maybe time had softened things and this might bring the family back together.

I met with my father at his house to get some pictures of mom. He told me he didn't want me to do it. He reminded me of the history of my sisters not supporting me and he was afraid I would get hurt again. I said I was doing it anyway. That's the thing about me. If I say I am going to do something, I do it. My word means everything to me. I hate people who say one thing and then do another. I see so many people who just live for their own comfort. I hate that. I am very aware of my place on earth and the passage of time. I feel when an opportunity to celebrate a rite of passage comes up, if you can honor it, you should. There are no guarantees about the future and that was something I saw time and time again as the years passed. This was something I wanted to do.

As in everything I do, I went to great lengths to make it very special. I went to the beautiful old stone Catholic church near my store and joined the parish so we could have it there. I hired a caterer and a bartender for the repast. I put together an elaborate invitation with "A Wonderful Life" theme. The front cover contained a collage of pictures of different photos taken throughout mom's life. I asked her friends to do readings and I wrote a heartfelt eulogy. I sent an invitation to everyone in my family including my sisters. I also invited all my mom's old friends. Kathleen's tribute to David's really touched me and I wanted mom's story to have many layers.

One of the best things that came out of my mom's memorial was that I reconnected with my godmother Lynn. Marilyn, or Lynn as she was known, was my mom's best friend in high school. The two girls were both Brooklyn Dodger cheerleaders and they grew up in similar circumstances. My mom served as godmother to Lynn's oldest child Lisa, and Lynn was my godmother. After my mom died in 1987 we kind of lost touch. I really wanted her to be a part of the event, but had no idea how to get in touch with her. The Internet allowed me to track her down. I found her ex-husband in a nursing home in Brooklyn. I placed a call to him and much to my surprise; he called back, even though he was in bad shape. He knew who I was and told me wonderful stories about my mother when she was young. I loved learning new things about her. It was a way of us connecting in my adult years and I so much longed for that.

He gave me the information I needed to get in touch with Lynn and I found her now living in New Jersey near the shore with her daughter Lisa. Lisa had epilepsy and was not able to work. Lisa married at 18 and was married a number of years, but after her marriage broke up she moved in with her mother. Epilepsy hit her hard and she really suffered with it. She was very beautiful and petite. I really liked her. When Lynn and I talked on the phone I learned that neither of them drove and since they were at least an hour away, I sent a car for them that day. Lynn had a second daughter, Allison. Allison and her husband Joe have two children and Lynn and Lisa had moved from Brooklyn to New Jersey to be closer to Allison. It was nice that they all lived near each other.

I planned the tribute to mom because I longed for a connection with my mother as adult. The depression I feel from her departure overwhelmed me at times and the longer she has been gone the more I miss her. Sometimes when I see a slim beautiful dark haired woman walking in

The Lonely Boy

the mall in front of me I still somehow hope it will be her. When they turn around and it's someone else I am always a little sad.

My mom wanted a closed casket and we honored her wishes, but in retrospect, I don't think it was a good thing for us. The last image I have of her is from Monday March 16th in the hospital bed. I never saw her after she passed and I think you often need that image so it can sink in. For many years after her death I would have a reoccurring dream that she never died and was transferred to another hospital somewhere far away for long term care in a vegetative state. In the dream, I found this out many years later and would go searching for her. I think the mind plays tricks on us. She went so quickly, three weeks from diagnosis to death. It was a lot to absorb.

I had really hoped that this memorial would give me some closure and maybe bring us all together as a family again. Hopefully my sisters would remember what was really important and who really brought us all together.

The invitation was beautiful and I sent it out around Valentine's Day against my father's advice and wishes. My Aunt Maria called right away and told me I should have had Jennifer on the cover as well. I guess you can't please everyone. I forgot that every time I got my family involved in something I did, it caused problems and created drama. Maybe my dad knew what he was talking about. I love music and I wanted to incorporate it into the event. The psychic I went to years earlier told me spirits often send messages to us through the lyrics in music and to listen to the signs. I wanted the music to be meaningful and reflective of her. Jennifer had sung a solo in grammar school. The song was called "On Eagles Wings." I knew Jennifer wouldn't do it and might not even come, so I asked a Katie, a friend of Marie's daughter to sing it.

Marie's daughter Gina had gone to school with a lovely girl named Katie. Gina and Katie were friends and neighbors with all of us in Bedminster. During her high school years, Katie lost both her mother and father to separate illnesses. Katie's aunt stepped in and took Katie and her siblings to Pennsylvania. But Katie hated it there and was very unhappy. Marie talked to Katie and offered to let her live with them so she could finish high school in Bedminster. The aunt challenged Marie on this and there was a battle. Marie's a very good hearted person, but she's also a fighter and she was tough. Somehow she got Katie out of Pennsylvania and raised her as her own daughter. Not only through high school, but also through college. That is why to this day I have such an affinity for Marie. She is such a good person, one in a million. Katie also looked like Jennifer at that age and I felt a synergy with her. She agreed and sang both that song and the "Ave Maria." My mother loved that sung in church. Another thing I did was to have parts of the mass sung. My Aunt Lil, who became so dear to me later in life, had her funeral mass sung by a distant family relative. I contacted my cousin Jill and got the same relative to come to sing parts of my mother's memorial mass. I asked everyone who came to wear something pink to honor women's cancers and to make us look united. I ordered 50 pink helium balloons and had them released in the grotto behind the church at the end of the service. Needless to say, it was over the top, but it was a time when I was doing very well and I wanted to do good things with my newfound prosperity. Today, I probably wouldn't been have been able to do it so lavishly.

As the invitations went out, unlike my 40th birthday, everyone in the family responded "yes," even my Brooklyn relatives who were never on board with anything I did. The only people who didn't respond were my two sisters. I know my dad had spoken to them, and my aunt did as well. They didn't care and wanted to spoil it. They never even considered my dad's shame as he walked into the church without his daughters.

This was our reality now. I hated it, but I wasn't going to live my life differently because of their hate. They were the ones missing out. When I booked the church, John mentioned jokingly, "What if it snows that day?" He followed up quickly by saying, "By March 18th the snow will be done." Well that morning there was a freak snow storm and I had to cancel at the last minute. I thought about karma again and wondered if this was a sign that I shouldn't have done it? But I rescheduled for the following

The Lonely Boy

Saturday. We lost some guests due to prior commitments, but it went perfectly. I am a very emotional person and really wanted to make a beautiful speech, but as we got closer to the event I realized I would probably break down. I didn't want this to be a second funeral. I wanted it to be a celebration of a beautiful life. I still had my tape recorder from the discrimination trial, so I taped my speech and had Father play it instead. It was a good call. It allowed me to be poignant without being morose.

The moment the car pulled up with my godmother and Lisa, all the fears I had about the day being a mistake were behind me. Everyone was so sweet and kind it exceeded my expectations. My favorite part was when we released the balloons. A little magic happened at that moment. I want to acknowledge that Marie's new boyfriend Bill was there and he even brought all the collages of my mom back to the house and set them up in my living room for the luncheon. He didn't know me very well and had never even met my mother, but he was very respectful and really helped that day. I began to see how loyal and respectful Bill was. He was a very good man and that's why Marie kept going back to him. I'm so glad she did. He became her caretaker in later years and stuck by her side no matter what. He was heaven sent.

I feel my mother's presence from time to time but I wondered if she was around that day. She once joked to my Aunt Maria that she would come back and haunt her. At one point when we were all telling stories about mom in my living room, a candle sconce popped off the wall unexpectedly and it made everybody jump. It would be just like my mom to have a little fun with us and let us know she was there. I hope she was.

After that event, my life changed a little. In her true selfless fashion I may have planned the tribute, but it was mom who left me with the gifts. My new insight into Bill led Marie and Bill to be our new go-to couple and brought new happiness for us. Carole Feltri, my mom's dear friend, did a reading that day. She and Don became newfound friends and our second new go-to couple. Best of all, I reconnected with my godmother Lynn who seemed to accept my lifestyle and she became a part of my life. On a little side note, as I was preparing for the repast, I always wanted a grandfather clock and Chippendale mahogany bench for the foyer, but could never afford them. Right before that day I found both in the same store for a ridiculously low price and had them in time for the repast. I wondered if that was mom too?

In December of that same year I threw my father a surprise 75th birthday party with a Christmas theme. When he turned 70, the rest of the family went to dinner without me and never told me, so we never really celebrated it.

Every time I had a psychic reading they always said something was going to happen to my dad. They told me to stay close to him and be good to him because I wouldn't

The Lonely Boy

have him for much longer and I needed to prepare myself. I always hoped it wasn't true, but I wasn't going to let another milestone birthday pass without a celebration.

I went down to Florida and stopped to visit Uncle Joe and Aunt Phil to invite them. I wanted dad to make peace with his brother and be in a better place, especially if it was coming to the end for him. I told them about the party and asked them to come. They were very cordial to John and I but they never showed. I invited them several times to things for my father but they never showed. It was something I could never fix for him. It was a big letdown because I loved them and I had really hoped we could move on after all those years.

We had 60 people anyway and it was very elegant. I was in the mall a few weeks before the party and I heard the most beautiful violin music coming from the center court. I walked towards the music and waited to talk to the violinist when he took a break. I hired him to come from New York on that Saturday night in December and he did a live Christmas concert for my dad's birthday in my house. The violinist alone cost almost $1,000 with the tip but it made the evening. I wore a new black cashmere jacket and vintage Ralph Lauren plaid Christmas pants. I had a private chef cooking in the kitchen and we had tons of staff and bartenders. I think I even had valet parking. It was very over the top. One of my guests told me she felt like she was in an episode of "Lifestyles of the Rich and Famous!" It

The Lonely Boy

would soon come to an end though and 2008 would bring us new worries and a sudden downturn.

The Lonely Boy

Chapter 12   Turning Point

We rang in 2008 with Don and Carole and Marie and Bill at our side, followed by a quick midnight phone call of good wishes to Lynn and her daughter Lisa. It started out as a good and prosperous year but by the fall of 2008, my design business started dropping off and the phone stopped ringing. Up until now I never had to look for business. In fact the only complaint I had from clients was that they had to wait a very long time to hear back from me. Things were suddenly different. We hadn't found a buyer for our Rocky Glen house and had rented it out, but the rent didn't cover the full mortgage and we now had a huge mortgage on the new house. We finally sold it, but it drained our savings.

Slowly I began to get concerned. And I was right to be concerned. The first bank to fail was the one we had our mortgage with. I wasn't surprised. They gave us a $1.3 million dollar bridge loan in a matter of days with no fuss. We were headed into an economic depression and I had to reinvent myself fast or we were going to be in trouble.

I decided to create Mavin Hill Painting, and I changed my marketing to focus on color consultation and painting. The word decorator became a bad word by 2009. I quickly saw how fast life could change as several houses on our street went into foreclosure. John and I cut back drastically and I started to do side jobs as well as consulting and working part time for a carpet store. 2010 rolled in and we were rocked when John lost his job of 17 years. Now with me barely working and John unemployed, we were in trouble.

Around this time, I began suffering from terrible headaches. I attributed them to the stress, but they kept coming on more frequently and seemed to be getting worse. I also started to notice I was having trouble seeing. I went to the eye doctor but she said everything in my eyes looked fine. I began to feel that things started looking dark to me. I went back to the eye doctor and she sent me to a neurologist. He sent me for a random CAT scan. At the end of the CAT scan, I could tell they found something. I asked them if they did and they reluctantly admitted they did. Both lab techs were holding my hands and were very careful with me. I knew it couldn't be good. The doctor sent me to a specialist at Robert Wood Johnson hospital to discuss my results. John had to drive me because of my loss of vision. He had a job interview in New Brunswick that day. He dropped me off and went to the interview. When the doctor came in, he was very blunt and said I had a massive and very aggressive brain tumor. I was shocked. He told me further that I would be blind shortly and that even when the tumor was removed I might remain blind for the rest of my life. He said the tumor was so big he didn't think he could get it all out. He said I would need radiation and he would have to cut me from ear to ear. There wasn't an ounce of compassion or empathy. He left the room and I was alone with my thoughts. At that moment, my longtime

The Lonely Boy

friend Malcolm called and kept me on the phone for 45 minutes until I calmed down. I as I got into car, John said, "How did it go?" I replied, "I can't believe I am saying these words, but I have a massive brain tumor." That night I rested and John informed everyone except for my father. John felt I should I should tell him myself. When I did, dad told me his mother had a brain tumor at the end of her life. They discovered it when she was in the nursing home.

My Aunt Maria was always great in a medical crisis and she quickly started research on brain tumors. Carole, who is also a great medical advocate, started making phone calls. We saw a lot of doctors. This was the worst thing John and I had ever been through together. We were barely paying the bills and now I was sick. John was doing side jobs and getting his severance package. I was still working but he had to be with me at all times. I was told DON'T DRIVE. There was a real dichotomy with Aunt Maria. On one hand she was calling three times a day with medical news. On the other, this is the same woman who said to me when I invited her to Thanksgiving one year, "If there's traffic on the bridge, we are just turning around." She attended every event with my sisters, but made it clear that she didn't want to be in my home. In fact, the Thanksgiving after my diagnosis, knowing I was sick, she went to Jennifer's house and never even told me. She called twice that day, but she never stopped by. She never even mentioned she was nearby. My dad ratted her out to me. It hurt me a great deal.

She did, however, give me the information that would save my life.

She found a doctor at New York Presbyterian Hospital who had developed an innovative procedure for my type of brain tumor. They go through the nasal cavity to the brain and deflate the tumor with the help of computers. I tried to get an appointment but the doctor was booked for weeks. I sent the doctor my CAT scans so he could see the severity of the situation. In the meantime, Carole also found me a surgeon at NYU who had had great success with brain tumors.

The doctor at NYU said that the tumor was too large and he thought I would be left with a partial tumor and still need have to have radiation. The guy had great credentials, but he looked about 13 years old. I liked him but I just wasn't sure. We sent my results to Mass General and to Johns Hopkins. My dad really wanted me to go to Johns Hopkins. When Dr. Schwartz of New York Presbyterian read my scan, he immediately set up an appointment for the following day. As soon as I pulled up to the hospital I felt good about it. It was Christmas time and the place was beautiful. With two story Christmas trees at the entrance, it looked more like a posh Upper East Side hotel than a hospital. When I met Dr. Schwartz, he was also young, but unlike all the other surgeons, he assured me that he could remove the whole tumor and that I wouldn't need radiation. He sent me to an eye specialist in the City to access the damage to my optic nerve and booked the appointment for surgery right after Christmas. Then something unexpected happened shortly after that visit. I woke up and I could barely see. I walked into our home office to tell John something was wrong. My eyesight was gone. I could only see shadows. Then we both felt a really cold breeze in the room. He said, "Did you feel that?" We checked to see if there was a window open. It was a Monday morning two weeks before Christmas. At that very moment, the phone rang. It was Dr. Schwartz's office. They said they had an opening and to come right now. Within an hour and a half, we were packed and at the New York Presbyterian emergency room. There was no bed available and I spent a day and a half on a gurney in the hallway blind, and most of the time alone. The slivers of light were so painful, I had to wear dark glasses just to control the pain. I am told the next morning Carole Feltri found out. She came to the hospital with my father to be there for him and for me. My father called Mary Anne and Jennifer and asked them to go to the hospital, but they refused. Carole got up at 4:30 in the morning to accompany dad so he would have a woman by his side for comfort. As they rolled me down the hall, I said goodbye first to Carole, then to dad, and finally to John. I realized this might be the last time I saw them and it was frightening. I could see through the slivers of light that John was going to lose it after I was out of sight.

The Lonely Boy

As I went under anesthesia, I remembered seeing a documentary about an operation where a woman woke up during a surgery, so I told the anesthesiologist to make sure he gave me enough anesthesia so I didn't wake up. It was my MMI, Marino Mental Illness, having its last dysfunctional say. That's the last thing I remember. I am told while I was under my dad specifically called Mary Anne and asked her to be with him. Carole told me she refused and that dad was crying. How could he have raised such a cold and vicious daughter? He was beside himself. The next thing I remember was opening my eyes. My vision was back. I vaguely remembering saying, "I can see. I can see again!!!!"

I spent the next week in intensive care. It was terrible. Kelly, my nurse, was very good to me but I couldn't ever sleep and the pain in my head was unbearable. I pushed the morphine button constantly. Good thing they control it. I would be dead right now otherwise. John and my father were there every night but it was a number of days before I could have other visitors. I remember hearing at the nurse's station that John's cousins Kevin and Jane were calling in one of my wake/sleep moments. One the third day, my Aunt Maria and Uncle Jack came to visit. Just as when I had my thyroid surgery, they were by my side. Even with all the bullshit, when I had a health crisis, they were both always there. Of course there were no sisters in sight, just

The Lonely Boy

like last time. Our Tewksbury neighbors had an empty condo on the Upper West Side and they offered to let John stay there while I was in the hospital, but he declined. I was so angry. One day in intensive care is like five normal days. The time goes so slowly and the drugs I was on were wreaking havoc with my depression. I was crying a lot. He didn't understand how awful this time was for me and what my brain was going through.

After a week, they put me in a regular room with another patient. He was very sick, and there were people in and out all day and night. My central line accidentally pushed out and I was gushing blood all over the floor. I screamed for help and it took a while for someone to help me. The level of care was not the same as in Intensive Care and I wanted to go home. They released me the next day. When John came to pick me up, he didn't get a wheelchair. They let me walk out. In fact, John made me in stand in line to pay for parking while he got the car. He had never had a health problem and had no idea how dizzy and how nauseous I was. When he finally drove up to the heated awning, I started having vertigo and got the spins very bad. It was bitterly cold and the combination of too much walking too soon and the rush of cold air did me in. It was just before Christmas and I think it was also a Saturday so we were stuck in massive gridlock. I had to put a scarf around my head to block the spins. It took over two hours to get home.

The Lonely Boy

When we got to the driveway, Marie and Bill were waiting for me. I didn't want to see anyone but they had been there for hours and she was the first person to see me. She had taken a turn for the worse and had developed Alzheimer's-like symptoms. She couldn't really communicate but she cried when she saw me. The goodness in her was still there even as she was starting to slip away from us. I thought to myself still with the scarf over my head, this is your core: John, dad, Carole and Don, Marie and Bill and maybe Uncle Jack and Aunt Maria. This was a painful but massive learning experience for me. Anyone who didn't come through for me now was dead to me. I spent my life giving and being kind to others. If people weren't there for me now, they were off the list. That evening food kept arriving along with gifts and flowers. It was overwhelming. I had mentioned once that I craved lasagna. I think I got four of them. I received so many good wishes and kindnesses; I was humbled by it all. The next morning was Sunday and I wanted to sleep as long as I could. I was exhausted and had had night sweats. I guess my body was detoxing from the anesthesia. I would have massive sweats and then wake up freezing in a pool of my own sweat. It was dreadful. This went on intensely for a week and continued milder for two weeks after that. I don't think John understood how sick I felt. I remember him saying he wanted us to go to his niece's for Christmas. I said, "I am not leaving this house."

The Lonely Boy

On Sunday morning, John came into the bedroom at about 9 am and told me my father was there. I said, "I want to sleep. Leave me alone." He insisted that I come down. I was wet with sweat and had a terrible headache. The strong smell of blood was in my nostrils and in my mouth. I still had packing in my nose because that's how they got to the brain. I was tired and very uncomfortable. But my dad was all charged up. He said, "I am going to bring the girls over this morning to see you." I said, "Dad, I am not up for this or them. Please just sit with me and keep me company. That's all I want right now." Well, he ran out the door and flew down my driveway. Now I was worried about him. It was the last thing I needed. I gave up on my sisters years ago. Mary Anne and Jennifer were done. I never wanted to see them again. I would only work with my core.

John tried to give me breakfast, but I couldn't eat. I also had not gone to the bathroom in over a week and they had John get me laxatives. I was a mess. About an hour later, I was laying down in the family room and John said, "Your dad is back, and he wants to see you in the living room." I said, "I don't want to get up." He insisted that I did but he did not join us. I saw that my dad was sitting in the large wing chair next to the piano with his coat still on. My dad said he was not coming to my house any more. I screamed, "What did I do to you?" He said, "I am tired of all this fighting between you all. You can come visit me if you want." He left in a huff. Later that afternoon my aunt called and I told her what had transpired. She said I am very worried about dad. "I'm afraid he is going to have either a heart attack or a stroke." She said that he was heartbroken that my sisters weren't there for me and that he felt responsible. She said, "What did you ever do them that was so bad to do this?"

I was upset for the rest of the day, and at about 8 pm that night I developed a bloody nose. The blood flow became quite steady. I panicked and we called the hospital. They said to lay back and do damp compresses and they told me that if I got light-headed, I should go to the emergency room. I told John I was not going back to a hospital and after an hour or so it began to stop.

That was the thing with my father. He loved me and was well intentioned, but he never wound up doing what was right for me. Without a wife he had made a lot of bad decisions and he wasn't at all in control. The next morning dad was the first person to call to see how I was feeling. Just like when my mom died and I came back home, I eventually realized he was unfiltered and that I needed to keep him at a safe distance.

Christmas Eve came and we did nothing. One of the neighbors dropped off lasagna and we had that for dinner. I was starting to feel hungry again and I really enjoyed it. John begged me to go to his niece's for a little while the next day. The trip takes about two hours each way when it's

The Lonely Boy

not a holiday. I told John I didn't think I could handle four to five hours in a car. But he persisted and I gave in.

His niece reminded me of my sister. She was cold and always wanted to be in control. As I lay on her downstairs sofa resting she was picking up wrapping paper and cleaning up. She didn't try to accommodate me or ask if I needed a blanket. I had to push John to leave because he loved being with his family, but we eventually left. All week we had company and more lasagna. John's two nephews sent us Broadway show tickets but his niece did nothing. Everyone else was super generous and I was almost embarrassed. As we rang in the New Year once again, Carole and Don, Marie and Bill and John were by my side. I think my dad went to a house party. Carole said to me at midnight, "2010 is behind you. Only good things are ahead." Later she sent me a beautiful card with those words and I have kept it on my desk ever since hoping her good wishes would change things for me. She is and always was a great cheerleader for me.

By the third week in January, I was bored and I started calling clients. I was worried about money, especially now with the multitude of medical bills and a 10-day stay in a New York City hospital.

John overheard me on the phone and he said, "What are you doing? You can't work yet!"

"We need the money," I said, "and I need to pull my weight."

The Lonely Boy

He took me on the client appointment and when the lady found out why John was with me she wanted me to go home and rest.

I am not someone who can lie on the couch and not be productive; I have anxiety disorder and depression. Work is therapy for me. I need to work. Not just for the money, but for the distraction. I had short bouts with anxiety before but it always went away. The last time though I needed medication. This time it was intense, and after I was diagnosed, it was a constant in my life. In fact, the morning I went into the hospital, I took my anti-anxiety pills and then a baby aspirin to prevent a heart attack because I was so stressed. On the way in, my aunt called. She said, "You can't take aspirin before brain surgery. Tell your doctor when you get there." She was right. They told me weeks earlier that I might need multiple blood transfusions. I was terrified of that. I said absolutely not. When I got there and told them I had taken an aspirin, they had to the start transfusions right away because I may have thinned my blood. I did not want a stranger's blood. I was incredibly paranoid about AIDS, especially being in a New York City hospital. They told me the blood supply was screened now and not to worry. I did anyway and it fueled my anxiety.

Over time, I slowly started getting back to work and I got a small design job in northwest New Jersey. I remember calling my dad as we were driving home. Dad said he loved the new color I recommended for his dining room. He had just painted the whole house himself and was thinking of selling. Dad and I had a simple but nice conversation and as he always did, he said "Thank you for calling." The psychic said he really appreciated all my checking-in since he had to chase down the girls to reach them.

It was the last time I would ever hear his voice again. The call was on a Thursday evening. I didn't call him on Friday but left a message on Saturday. On Sunday, I had one of my painters at the house and was distracted with a problem. That's when I got a call from Jennifer. It was around 2:30 pm. Dad had a massive stoke. She said, "Just get to the hospital."

John and I ran out the door and flew to the hospital. In the car, I called my aunt and uncle. They flew just as fast from Brooklyn. When I got there, Mary Anne and Jennifer and Mary Anne's asshole husband were there. Jen had divorced Mark so I think she was alone, but I'm not sure. There was no acknowledgement of my health or wellbeing. They just stated the facts and it was evident that the sequence of events was very much staged and they had been there for hours. The doctors came in and told us it didn't look good. Apparently, I was the last one to talk to dad. Sometime in the middle of that Thursday night, he had had the stroke. Jennifer found him Sunday morning when they were supposed to have had breakfast together. Records indicated that an ambulance was called by 9 am. I was not notified until 2:30 pm. John and I knew what was happening. Norm,

The Lonely Boy

Mary Anne's husband, mentioned that he was going to keep an eye on the house, but at that point, I was only concerned with my dad's survival. About an hour later my aunt and uncle arrived. It was very sad and we all cried except Mary Anne who never showed any emotion. It was clear she wanted to be in control.

I had no faith in her or love for her anymore. My fear for my father's life kept me from feeling all the rage I had for these two witches who caused my father to have the stoke my aunt predicted six weeks earlier. Norman acted like he was the head of command and it disgusted me. Norman said we better get a hold of Uncle Joe. Dad's brother was older and in Florida. You don't call old people with bad news until you know all the details. "What a useless moron," I thought

While they were playing games, I spoke to the doctors myself. I asked if I could get a copy of dad's CAT scan. I explained that I just had surgery and I had a renowned neurologist who was willing to look at my dad's scans.

When I left New York Presbyterian, Dr. Schwartz gave me his cell phone number and told me to call him anytime I had a problem. I called and I told him about my father. He told me he would meet me the next day before office hours to read my dad's CAT scan, but that he needed the films tonight. I asked my aunt and uncle who were going back to New York to drop them off and they left with them shortly after.

The Lonely Boy

The next day, John and I got up early and drove into the city. Dr. Schwartz was already waiting for us. He said, "I am not going to lie to you. It's bad, however, he could live a long time with the brain the way it is." He said dad might have problems, especially with speech, but that it was too early to tell. Knowing that we were probably not looking at imminent death, we went back to the hospital. We had just realized was it was Valentine's Day, so we scarped down a piece of pizza quickly in the hospital parking lot and moved on.

Dad was stable for a few days but then developed a staph infection with a high fever. As I was cooling him with ice chips, Mary Anne came in and we asked her for a key to dad's house. She was evasive and she and John had words. She called Norman and the bully came in and starting fighting with us in front of my very sick father. I had to calm that piece of shit down because I didn't want my father to have a second stroke. When he finally left, John and I came to the conclusion that they had cleaned out the house before they even called us.

The hospital admitted dad in the morning. We weren't notified until 2:30 pm. They had a plan in action. They were very jealous of our success and this was going to be a power trip for the losers to cause problems.

At one point I said to Norman, "I can't have all this stress. I'm recovering from brain surgery." He replied, "We know about your problems." I wished God struck him dead right there. This man was evil incarnate—the reason my father lost his family and, I fully believed, the reason he had the stroke. After we left that night, I decided to email Mary Anne. I asked for no more Norman around my father and I didn't see him again at the hospital. He apparently was spending all his time cleaning out my father's house.

Before my father was off the ventilator, his doctor asked me to find out what his wishes were, and to see if they could have it in writing. I called his lawyer the next day and was told that dad only had a will. In the will, he left all his assets to his three children equally. There was no power of attorney, no living will, and no special instructions. The Executor of the will was his lawyer so no one was in charge. I took copies of what I had learned for both my sisters but felt that evil jealous Mary Anne already had something else in play. She was too sure of herself and not at all fazed by her father's mortality.

Dad was a fighter, I knew that. If there was a chance he would make it, he would. He was very strong emotionally and physically. When he came off the ventilator, I asked the doctor if we could start therapies as soon as possible. Aunt Maria and I were doing nonstop research and the doctor said if dad continued to be stable they would consider moving him to another facility. Mary Anne worked for a health insurance company and she insisted putting him in a nursing home where she knew all the people. I strongly disagreed. I found out that there was a great Brain Trauma Unit at JFK Medical Center in nearby Edison. They made wonderful progress with stroke patients who started therapy early and didn't have other underlying health issues. Mary Anne was pushing for a nursing home. I said no.

The doctor agreed with me and dad was moved to JFK. I accompanied him in the ambulance and John followed me in the car. The BTU was very sterile and strict with padded locked doors.

After we checked him in, I learned that we couldn't visit until the weekend. Then they asked me for hard copies of paperwork and more insurance information, but I had none. I had been locked out of the house. In the beginning, they want no distractions. So we honored that and we didn't see dad for the rest of the week.

The next time I visited him he looked pretty good. He was upright in his wheelchair and recognized me right away. When I spoke to the doctors they were very positive and hopeful. They told me dad was still very tired but felt he had potential. Dad kept trying to tell me something. He would make noises that sounded like "nor, nor, nor." I think he was trying to say Mary Anne's husband's name, Norman. I asked him to write it but he couldn't. What was he trying to tell me? The staff suggested I come to some of his therapies to encourage him and I did just that. I was surprised to see how much he comprehended. He actually got angry when some of the things they asked him to do seemed juvenile, like pointing to a picture of a duck. We were all very encouraged by his progress. The next night I wasn't feeling well but I called to see how he was doing. The nurse said Mary Anne put a password on his file and told them she was his guardian. She didn't tell me that or give me the password. I had to email her and wait until she got back to me.

I knew she was pulling something. She had stolen all the paperwork from his house and because she came forward with it first, they made her the point of contact. That's when I knew there was a problem. They were still hiding something and wouldn't give me a key to the house.

I made an appointment with the social worker at the hospital. She said, "I've met people like Mary Anne before. She cleaned out the house, locked you out and went through your dad's checkbooks to see how much money he had." She said, "You better get a lawyer."

From that day forward, all information was filtered through my sister. I had no direct access to any of the doctors. She then told me the insurance was done and they were moving him into a nursing home—one, I determined, where she could pull all the strings. I tried to get the insurance company to grant an extension, but she wouldn't go along. On the day dad was scheduled to leave, he developed blood clots. After a stroke, this is often the second round that causes death. I called in a favor at Robert Wood Johnson Hospital where I knew someone, and we had a filter put in to prevent him from dying. While they were doing it, Mary Anne insisted on putting her name first on the release. Emails came from her daily, but all of them were about putting him in a nursing home, not rehabilitating him. John and I decided to go to the house to see if the social worker was right. We jimmied our way in through the back door. It was obvious that dad's home office and all the valuables had been sloppily ransacked. Everything was gone. There was even an empty file on dad's desk labeled, "John and Rich" and it was empty. Why did they want our building records? This was bad.

John and I went back the next afternoon and saw that Mary Anne and Jennifer were taking the hallway wallpaper down. I emailed them and asked them to stop. I wrote, "When dad comes home he'll need things to be as familiar as possible."I knew I wasn't dealing with people that had his best intentions at heart. I was doing therapies with dad and trying to save his life while they were concerned about taking wallpaper down. After they refused to stop I called the local police department. They said it was a family matter and they wouldn't get involved. I asked for a copy of the police report when the 911 call came in and the police came to the house the day they found dad on the floor. They told me there wasn't one.

There's always a police report when someone is taken out of a house. The girls admitted they called the police and an ambulance and that they were there when emergency services got there. Why was there no record of it? What was the police connection?

Why wasn't I called from the scene right then and there? Now I knew I was dealing with corruption and criminals. I spoke to my aunt about how to proceed and she suggested that we meet in person at JFK Hospital to figure out what was going on and decide what to do next. John drove me but stayed in the lobby. The three of us went into the coffee shop off the lobby. Mary Anne had become empowered and was very confident at that meeting. She said, "I'm in charge now and you'll do what I tell you to." I said, "I want him to continue stringent therapies." I told her I went to the VA hospital to investigate options and learned that when dad came home, they would pick him up and drop him off for therapy three days a week for free.

She said she had already enrolled him at the nursing home. I raised my voice and said, "Congratulations. You have completely destroyed this family." As I walked away, ungrateful, selfish Jennifer yelled back, "No, you did."

John was worried about my health so we just left. Mary Anne and Jennifer went to Security and reported me as having attacked them and said they wanted to press charges. The security guard said, "Ma'm, you are alone here." I found this out the next day when the social worker told me what the two evil girls tried to pull.

Once he was in the nursing home, I no longer received any information on my dad's well being. Soon afterwards, I

The Lonely Boy

was served papers in my driveway. My sister was suing for legal guardianship of my dad. The court server saw how upset I was and said, "When I come to a house like this and see a sibling suing, it's always over jealousy."

About a week or so after that, I received a phone call. The call on my cell phone was from a former police captain in the town where my dad lived. He told me he was a friend of my sister's. He said he was put on the case as the temporary guardian. He said he was going on vacation and because he already knew her he was putting her in charge while he was on vacation. He said, "And by the way, I know you don't get along because you're gay." I was shocked and horrified. This was the set-up and the police connection that made her so confident. I processed what this man said and called him back. I said I wanted an independent party involved and I didn't want dad's therapies interrupted. He complied for the moment and a friend of his supposedly covered for him while he was on vacation. Now, I knew I needed a lawyer. I had not worked in a long time and John still wasn't working either. How could we afford a lawyer? Carole gave me the name of a good lawyer and I went to see him.

He was very aggressive and said, "We are going to hit her and hit her hard." He told me it would cost about a $100,000 and that he would need 20 percent down. I left horrified. I had $10,000 liquid and I borrowed the other $10K from my SEP IRA. I sent him the liquid $10K the next day telling him the rest would follow. Two days later I got my $10K check back. "You can't afford me," he wrote. When he saw that I couldn't give him the whole deposit at once, he dropped me. I re-deposited it. Everywhere I went, it was the same: a huge expense with no guarantees. Carole found another attorney named Dale. He had gone out socially with my parents and knew of them. He was a devout Christian and said he would help me. I gave him a $5,000 retainer and we got started.

All the stress was not good for my health, and my follow-up MRI showed it. I had severe scarring in my brain. I had a slight hearing loss and my vision was never as good as it had been, but I had to suppress that or I might be ruled an unfit guardian. What a mess dad left me.

Dale and I had to start working on dad's case right away. My main concern was making sure that all of dad's therapies—physical therapy (PT), occupational therapy (OT), and speech therapies—would be continued. I had been doing a great deal of research on dad's condition and how to heal him. My Aunt Maria gave me so much help with this, but she also hurt me very badly. At one point, she actually said, "I'll help you, but I don't want anyone knowing I'm helping you." It really disgusted me. She was trying to keep my sisters in her good graces for herself and her daughter, but at the same time she knew they were doing something very wrong.

The Lonely Boy

That previous Thanksgiving, she had called me several times knowing I was very sick with my brain tumor, but she went to Jennifer's house for dinner and didn't even stop by to visit. I knew I couldn't trust her, but I needed her support so I continued to engage her for dad's sake. Mary Anne had obviously made a deal with this former police captain and I needed all hands on deck if I was going to help dad and keep him out of a nursing home permanently.

I sought out the best people in the medical field to help me make my case. I had a friend who was an administrator at Robert Wood Johnson and he found me a medical doctor who specialized in geriatric care. He would examine my dad to determine where he was in his recovery and how to proceed from there. Dale, my attorney, found a Licensed Care nurse to write a professional plan of care. I had her meet with dad several times under the guise of being a family friend. I also had dad's psychologist testify—she knew my sisters and my dad's mental state. Finally, I hired a speech therapist who worked at the Adler Center to examine him and to testify about how important therapies were for him. I reached out to every family member and every friend that dad had. So many people came forward I had to have two meetings. The first was at my house, and the second wave was at Dale's office.

Thirty people, mostly friends of my dad's, came to the meeting at the house. They knew what the girls were doing was shady and they were going to back me all the way. The second round was at Dale's office, and 12 more people showed. It was quite obvious what my sisters were plotting. How could a family court judge not know what was going on here?

Dale and I submitted interrogatories to explain our positions. I explained how unhappy I was that the nursing home wouldn't give me any information on dad's care. I also outlined my vigorous plan of therapy based on the information I received from the professionals who met him. I asked that my dad be removed from the nursing home ASAP.

The day after I submitted the court paperwork, I received a note at the desk of the nursing home. The general manager, Mary Anne's buddy, had threatened to sue me for writing about my dad's care. He even threatened to restrict my visits. So I called dad's temporary guardian to complain. Mary Anne had obviously taken my interrogatories to the nursing home to harass me. The temporary guardian called me back and said Mary Anne didn't do it, he did. This guy was evil, and he was messing with me. All of my dad's therapies were stopped the next day. He never has had therapy again.

One day I happened to pass the house dad bought as an investment for some extra income in retirement. There was a "for rent" sign in the window with Norman's cell phone number. I was never notified even though I was a licensed real estate agent and his only son. I knew I was being defrauded. I contacted every agency I could think of to help, but I always got the same answer. It's a family matter. You need to get a good lawyer at your own expense. I must have heard that a hundred times.

I contacted the news media and spoke with Sarah Wallace from ABC Channel 7 and one of the field reporters from Fox News. In the end, they were afraid of a lawsuit and backed out. I was trapped in a perfect storm. My sisters were set on a course of action that would ruin dad's life and I was going to do everything in my power to stop it.

The nursing home wanted to supervise my visits with dad now, so I was very careful when I was there. I asked the temporary guardian if I could have a doctor examine dad to see if therapies should be resumed. He refused. This guy was Mary Anne's advocate. I knew was going to need to pull some tricks quickly or I was going to lose.

I found a top doctor willing to help, and I waited until the Fourth of July in the evening to sneak him in to give dad a physical. It worked, and the doctor's report was filed. When the guardian found out, he went to the nursing home management to try to get me banned from seeing my father. I had to meet with the general manager and listen to their side. I was in Mary Anne's territory now and I was out of ammunition. My only hope was that Dale could get the temporary guardian removed and replaced with an impartial third party.

The Lonely Boy

The stress of this was not good for me and I was still suffering from nerve damage and headaches. John said at one point, "It's obvious that Mary Anne made a deal with the devil. Maybe you need to let it go. Your dad wouldn't want you to get sick over this." He was right and we both knew it, but I had to keep trying. I didn't want to look back on my life and feel like I let him down. I had to try even though I pretty much knew the deck was stacked against me.

In June we went to family court for the preliminary hearing. I found out through Facebook that my sister and the temporary guardian were Facebook friends. There was a previous relationship and we requested that the temporary guardian to recuse himself. In less than five minutes, I could tell that the judge and the former police captain were working as a team. The temporary guardian even acknowledged that he had had a previous relationship with Mary Anne, but the judge would not recuse him. I left that day with a keen understanding of why she was positive she'd win the case. She made some kind of deal.

I kept a low profile at the nursing home but was very worried about dad's therapies being abandoned. He was so much stronger at JFK. He could wheel himself around quickly when he wanted to. He was eating vigorously and despite the wheelchair, looked like a young healthy guy. I believe as you get older it becomes easier to see the truth. Life experience helps you cut through the crap and see what's real because you have lived long enough to know how life plays out. For me, truth is the deciding factor which establishes right or wrong. I saw the truth about my father. My dad couldn't speak, but when you saw him you knew the truth that he was a healthy man that had one quick blip in his life. This blip would change his life, but not end it. He had a strong heart and lungs from working all those years in construction. This man needed to go back to his own home with a full-time live-in aide and begin rebuilding his damaged but salvageable life. When you saw him in those early days walking with a walker and trying to talk, you saw his truth. I couldn't walk away from that. It was just too obvious.

Before we went to trial, I stopped by dad's house and my dad's next door neighbor was sitting out on a lawn chair. She was in her 80s and had slight dementia. She had a full-time live-in aide with her. Angie remembered me and kissed me. She even asked how old I was. I said, "I feel so old." She said, "You don't look old."She was still pretty good then. Her aide said, "Bring your dad home, we can put them out together. Angie would love the company." In the hope I would prevail in court, I found a really great full-time live-in aide. She had all her credentials. She was a U.S. citizen and was great with dad. I showed up with her twice at the nursing home claiming she was a family friend. She had great chemistry with dad. She even cooked for him one day. I knew in my heart this was the right thing for him. It wouldn't be an easy life for me running back and forth to New Brunswick, but it was what I had to do.

When the trial started, Carole picked me up every day. I was driving now but not all the time. On the first day of court I had so many people with me they had to bring more chairs in. Once again, in the first five minutes, it was very clear that we were going through the motions so Mary Anne could get legal claim to the money she had already taken from the house. On the night before the trial, Mary Anne's counsel accidentally sent me a copy of her plan of care. Her plan of care was done the night before trial. She apologized to her lawyer for waiting so long to put together a plan of care. This all but proves that for Mary Anne, it was never about Henry E. Scuderi's well being at all. It was all about defrauding me and being able to legally start spending my father's money. The first line read, "I would like to control my brother right from the start with restricted or supervised visits." There was no plan of care with respect to therapy of any kind. The plan, it seemed, was to give her legal access to all of his money and leave him in the nursing home for the rest of his life with no chance of getting better.

I knew now more than ever that I had to try to save him. The only thing I could hope for now was that maybe Jen loved him and when she heard from a doctor who testified that it was imperative that he resume therapies it would get to her. According to my books and the research I did on strokes, every day he didn't receive therapy it was setting him further back. There is a clear window with these things and we needed to get him going again. It perplexes me that they would give up on him so easily, especially Jennifer, who was now a gym teacher. Jen had become very fit in later years and you'd think she would be on board with this. When I took the witness stand later that day and I saw my two sisters sitting there, I decided to give it one last try to stop all of this. After I was sworn in, I reached out to them and said I loved my sisters and that we needed to stop this proceeding and work together to bring him home. It wasn't a ploy, it was truth and you can't hide truth. The judge could see I was telling the truth, and Mary Anne's counsel went crazy. This gave me credibility in the eye of the court. How do you tear down someone who just told you he loved you?

When we broke for lunch, the temporary court guardian said to Mary Anne outside, "We'll get him on the next round." My words fell on deaf eyes. These girls were evil and they were in it for the money. They didn't want him to speak again. Dad must have witnessed them taking all the cash out of the house while they were waiting for the ambulance. Dad kept saying "nor, nor, nor" to me because he was warning me that Norman took his cash and rifled through his things. That's why they were both in on it, and that's why they never wanted him to speak again. Why else would any child fight to stop speech therapy for their father??? It was because of what that had done. They could be implicated in a felony and potentially go to prison.

When we came back from lunch Mary Anne's legal team grilled me and tried to make me out as having a bad relationship with my father. I said, "I don't care what you try to manipulate. I love my father and what you are doing here is wrong." They brought up the note from 1999 stating that John and I owed dad $10,000. I explained that we returned it. I had the paper trail of checks and told them that in the end, dad wrote off the balance of the loan as a gift, just as he had given a gift to his other children when they got married. The judge said he was fine with that and no other questions were asked about it.

The next morning started with the medical witnesses and Dr. Malik took the stand. He was very passionate about my dad and spoke in detail about his health and how he was a prime candidate for therapy. He said stopping therapy wasn't only a mistake, it was a crime. It got very heated. He said what they were doing was basically killing him. The judge shut him down and threatened to have him put in jail. Every other medical professional—the registered nurse, the psychologist, and the speech therapist—spoke of the merits of continuing therapy and home care.

The next day, the family witnesses took the stand and Aunt Maria decided she had to testify. She made it painfully obvious that she wasn't defending or siding with me in any way, but she said they had to continue with dad's therapies. She said she just felt very strongly that no therapy was a very wrong decision. When she got off the stand, Jennifer called her aunt an explicative and the two walked out. Maria left and it was a bad scene.

The next day in the morning on the way to court I called Aunt Maria to see how she was doing. She was very nasty to me. She said not to use her name in anything I said. She blamed me for what my sisters did and said. She told me that her daughter was not going to have a relationship with her cousins anymore because of me. Really?

Thursday was the last day of testimony and the judge told us he would not be in on Friday for personal reasons. That gave me the whole weekend to be anxious about a Monday decision. I knew it was all rigged. I drove out to the Carmelite Monastery in Flemington that Saturday to pray for dad's well being. I was pretty sure I wouldn't win. Even the home health aide I hired told me, "This is rigged. It will never happen." My cousin Sylvia said it was rigged. "This is corruption," she said. My side of the courtroom was packed with medical professionals, all dad's friends, and the rest of the extended family. My sisters had only their husbands and Mary Anne's mother-in-law on their side. They had no plan of care, no provisions for quality of life, and they had illegally taken all of my father's assets with no authority or permissions.

Monday came and we all rose. The judge said, "We have a brother and sister that both want to help their father. They are equal to me, but the son could owe the father money so I am giving the sister guardianship." It was the biggest betrayal of my life. We left the court and as we walked to the car. I felt the sting of discrimination more painfully than ever before in my life. When we got home, Carole and Don stayed with us and John made us all a nice meal. John said, "I want you to put all this behind you and move on with your life. It's over. Focus on your business and your health." I understood all that but I also knew the shenanigans were only starting. This whole episode was fueled by the jealously Mary Anne and Norman had for me. This was never about my father. It was personal. This was her way of saying, "I am still better than you." She never realized she caused my father to have a stroke and then left him to die a long slow lonely death in an institution. That night she and the other criminal wrote an email gloating about their win. The following week they filed a motion to deny my request for reimbursement of my legal fees. The court said my defense was meritless and a waste of time. They got away with that too. Dale continued to work for me for the rest of the ordeal and he did much of the work pro bono. He told me at 75 this was the worst case of corruption he had ever seen.

Next, the stealing started. Mary Anne tried to sell herself the home dad had purchased as an investment and she used my parents' lifesavings to fund her scheme to take it for her own gain. I won that round, but it wreaked havoc on my mental health. When I left the court that day, I drove myself to 185 Baldwin Street. It was the two family house where our lives began. I parked out front and sat there for a while. I tried to remember a time when we were all a family and all I felt from my family was love and safety. How could all the good my parents did go so horribly wrong?

The court cases continued and the stealing went on for many years. At one point I received an email from Mary Anne telling me that I had one hour to meet her at the house to see what I wanted from dad's things. When I agreed on a time, she told me the temporary guardian, who was now off the case, decided he wanted to be there too. He and she would decide what I would or wouldn't get. When it occurred to me that for all I knew the guy could plant drugs on me or set me up in some way, I made the decision not to go. I walked away with nothing. I don't have a cup, a dish or a single picture from a lifetime on Clifton Avenue. I am sure all of my dad's tools are in Norman's basement even though I am my father's only son.

One day I passed 21 Clifton Avenue where I spent my entire childhood and I noticed there was a wheelchair ramp out front. For a brief moment, I thought, "Oh my God, she finally did the right thing and brought him home." Then it hit me. There were strange cars in the driveway. She sold our family home and the court didn't even have to tell me.

The Lonely Boy

Now some other disabled person would be able to live in peace in the house my father built for all of us.

On a Sunday a few months later, John and I went to visit my father in the nursing home and his bed was empty. When I called the desk, I was told my dad had been moved to the hospital days before. I received no phone call or notification. The woman at the desk told me that my sister instructed them not to tell me anything. When we rushed to St. Peter's Hospital, the staff told me that he had a life threatening blood clot in his leg and that they were instructed not to tell me anything. This doctor added that he hoped Mary Anne wouldn't be mad for telling me as much as he did. I couldn't believe my ears.

When I got to his room, dad was in pain and was clearly distressed. He wouldn't look at us. He was just staring at the ceiling. I asked the nurse why he didn't have television. She said my sister said it wasn't necessary. I pulled out my credit card to get television set up for him and I put it on before we left. As I went to hug him goodbye, he swung at me and hit me in the face. I left feeling more alone than I'd ever felt in my life.

With each subsequent court case, I got more and more disillusioned with life and I lost my faith in humanity. Aunt Maria's husband called the house one day and left a message saying that they were walking away from me. I never saw or heard from them again. Now defrauded and discriminated, I was truly done with family. I began to feel

The Lonely Boy

hate in my heart and that's not really who I am. Dad kept getting weaker and weaker. My attorney suggested we try one last appeal with a new judge. When I met him at the courthouse, he looked at me and I realized I just couldn't handle it anymore. It was too damaging for me. I just had to give up and accept that my father could not be helped.

I had reached a point where I could no longer deal with the evil. I had to separate myself from it. I began having panic attacks and my depression kicked in with a vengeance, worse than ever before. The same year my dear friend Rick died of heart related problems at only 47. My godmother's daughter Lisa developed lung cancer and we also lost her a short time later, on Christmas morning. As I saw this beautiful young woman in the casket, I thought of my own sweet mother who was about the same age when she passed. She was taken from us way too soon and it just broke my heart. From that moment on I kept Lynn close to me and we have become family. Lynn's remaining daughter Allison came up to me in church at the end of the funeral and told me she always wanted a brother. She very much made that happen and we've slowly became family to each other.

For the next few years I focused on my business. I still visited my father all the time but I threw myself into my work. Ironically, I had the opportunity to open up a retail store in the town where Mary Anne and Norman lived and I did. My focus was on work and my dad. I'd spend Sunday

The Lonely Boy

afternoons with my father who was now in a vegetative state, and then have dinner with Marie who was also in a vegetative state. Bill had become her fulltime caregiver. It was just so sad I couldn't stand it. I wasn't built to handle all the sadness in the world, but I am a survivor. This time, however, it overwhelmed me and one night while John was away I had a psychotic episode and woke up in the morning on the bathroom floor. I felt I needed in-patient treatment in a hospital. John made some phone calls and I was told my best bet was medication and therapy. I went to see a psychiatrist and was diagnosed with severe depression and anxiety. I went on medication and rocketed from 177 pounds to 214. I also started seeing a therapist on a weekly basis. This was truly my darkest hour. I was afraid I would never be Richard Scuderi again. I didn't think I could ever be normal. The panic attacks were severe and the depression was often overwhelming. I found it odd that I could be on depression meds and still be very depressed. The weight gain was an added delight which of course made me more depressed. There it was: my life had come full circle, and once again I was at the bottom.

The Lonely Boy

Chapter 13   Healing and Spiritual Enlightenment

As we rang in 2015, I was with my core once more, my partner John, Carole and Don, and Marie and Bill. Marie was in a wheelchair now. I continued to visit with dad but every time I left I felt sick. I felt he must have thought we sold him out. John wanted me to talk to dad and tell him what had really happened with the trial, but I couldn't. It would only hurt him to know what had transpired. Also, after the last appeal, there was nothing that anyone could do. I didn't want to put that burden on someone who had nothing left. He had suffered enough. I tried to distract myself with work and other things. Then I suddenly realized I was going to be turning 50 in April. The depression medication blew me up. I didn't to be 50 and fat. I decided I wanted to be my best self. So I started working out every day to get in shape. I also cut out flour and sugar from my diet. I have always struggled with my self esteem, so I wanted to make sure I felt confident that day. I had hoped the pictures would capture a 50-year-old Richard that looked more like 40.

I came up with a great theme: we'd have a 1960s "Mad Men" party. All the guests would wear their 60s best. The menu would feature beef wellington, coq au vin and Jell-O molds. I used my parents' 1964 wedding pictures for my inspiration. I did everything in yellow and white as they did including a two-tiered fondant cake made by a pastry chef from the Culinary Institute. From the driveway entrance and throughout the house, every detail was perfect. I shopped until I found the perfect form-fitting 60s-inspired black suit, the perfect narrow gray and white necktie from Burberry's and amazing 60s-inspired black patent leather shoes. I lost all the weight I'd hoped to lose and I must admit I thought I looked pretty good. I was told just that by many people that night.

I was still carrying a lot inside and I felt the diversion of the party would help me get through this milestone in my life. None of my immediate family would be there, only friends and John's family. On my actual birthday, I brought a small cake to the nursing home that I wanted to share with my dad. There was a new nurse on duty that day. She was very nasty to me. She said, "What do you want, to kill him with that cake?" I asked her to get him a pudding instead and I fed it to him. I took out the candles out of the cake, and gave it to the staff. No matter what I did now, nothing would ever be the same with dad and I had to just accept that.

The weather on the day of the party couldn't have been more perfect. The house looked gorgeous filled with yellow spring flowers. I hired a piano player and he played Burt Bacharach tunes. It was just perfection. We had about 60 people there, but the house could handle it. We had an open bar and it was packed. It was mostly friends, but we invited John's family too and they all came. I booked rooms at a

The Lonely Boy

local hotel and arranged for gift bags and a shuttle to take people back and forth. It was extravagant, but after all I had been through I felt I needed it. When John's sister arrived, she told me she had a gift I really needed and kept going on about it. I saw her chuckling with her daughter in the corner. I always felt that John's middle sister was jealous of us, especially when she came to our house for parties. I overheard her say to Carole and Don, "I don't know why they need such a big house?"

I made sure I spoke to every guest and spent time with them that night. When I got to John's niece, I thanked her for coming and told her I had gotten a two-night comp in Atlantic City. John and I went often and so did she and her husband. We were often there at the same time but never together. I wanted to give her one night of the comp, so we could all go together. John has always wanted to be closer to his niece, but most times when John invited her to things she was too busy. I know that hurt John. I was actually surprised she even came to my party. So in the spirit of the evening, I told her we wanted us to be closer to her and your husband. She said, "That's impossible. I love John, but I don't approve of your relationship." Then she basically proceeded to tell me off. When I opened the gift that John's sister and niece told me I needed so desperately, it was a selfie stick. Another put-down, just like when my old pal Frank gave me the book "If Life is a Bowl of Cherries, What am I Doing in the Pits?" when I turned 16.

The Lonely Boy

At 50, I was still surrounded by people who were bad for me and wanted to hurt me. I was so upset by that.

I decided that I needed to do some soul-searching to try to find out why my life always led me to bad people that left me with angst and self doubt. I needed to find out why I was so unhappy. I just couldn't handle the pain any more. I decided if I was going to continue to live, I didn't want to do it with depression and anxiety any more. I was tired of being on medication. I was tired of all the side effects of depression. I often had belabored breathing, nausea and trouble sleeping. I used to have a drink before I left the house for any social event just to relax me. I didn't want a drink, I needed one. The feelings of despair and sadness plagued me throughout my day and getting through even one day was mentally and physically exhausting. I needed to come up with a new life strategy.

Being the nice guy all these years may have made points with my maker, but it had done little for me in on earth. I am someone who feels things very deeply. I used to think that it was a gift, but now I find it a mixed blessing. I want to take the rest of my life and only do things that are rewarding to me. I want to finally be at peace with myself.

I started slowly by getting the people out of my life that didn't have my best interests at heart. I began to evaluate my friendships and relationships and focused on the people who brought positive energy into my life. I let go of the ones who brought me grief. I didn't fight with them or cause them pain, I just let those relationships slip away. This helped me overcome my anxiety and depression. I turned toward my faith in God and I started to pray. I asked for his guidance in my troubled and painful life journey. I believe faith in God can really bring peace.

I reconnected with some of the people that made me happy in the past. I reunited with Dawn on her 50th birthday and we had a great dinner together. I made my old friend Jeannie a part of my life again and it brought me good memories of the past to draw on. Jeannie brought new people into my life. They were positive and supportive and they taught me about meditation which in turn started to help me with some of the discomfort I felt in my own body because of mental distress. I also put new energy into old friendships with wonderful people like my friend Audrey. She is one of my most loyal friends and she has always been a good force in my life.

I began talking to people about my depression and anxiety—the MMI/Marino Mental Illness I mentioned earlier. Aunt Maria once told me she had belabored breathing too, so I guess it is something I inherited. Realizing that we both carried this burden somehow made it less scary for me now and it explained what I was going through. I know Uncle Jack and Aunt Maria are very good people and I hope one day to have them in my life again. I accepted that our challenges were fueled out of joint dysfunction, not hate. When you finally make peace with your truths, it's very freeing. There is such a stigma with mental illness and it's particularly hard for men to admit we have a problem. We feel it makes us seem weak and diminishes our power. For me, however, knowing that other people know that I was not always feeling right helped me to feel much less anxious.

I accepted that what happened to my dad was out of my control, just like a lot of things in life. I did the best I could and I began to forgive myself for not being successful in my effort to help him. The cards were stacked against me. These were crimes my sisters committed and one day they will have to account for their sins.

I also adjusted to the changes in my father as he slowly declined. I put on a brave face and did my best to let him know he was still very much loved and appreciated. The hardest thing that I have been working on is forgiving my sisters. I can't tell you that I'm not sad and angry that Jennifer has two sons that I will never know and my sweet nephew Michael, Mary Anne's son, is now a grown man. I'm not built for such sadness. I had to let it go. It was just hurting me too much. I had to forgive them for my own mental well being.

In an effort to find peace and closure, I decided to have another psychic reading. There were just too many unanswered questions in my life. In a recent reading, supposedly my mom came through. She said, "Just let go and throw it all to the wind." I did just that. I decided to focus now on what I was good at and what made me happy.

In 2016, I opened two more Mavin Hill Design locations and they have become pretty successful. I hired interns and started mentoring them. I started a small local radio show called Modern Design where each week I interview people on current design topics and I use my broadcasting degree in conjunction with my design background.

John and I just celebrated our 23rd year together and two days before Christmas 2016 we married in a simple ceremony in front of the fireplace in our living room. We have learned from our previous experiences with family and just kept it private. We decided to accept the things we cannot change and to move forward together. Finally, and this is critical for me, I realized that the struggles I faced all my life were not just mine. Yes, very bad things happened to me, but I am not alone. We are all here on a journey to redeem ourselves. No one gets out of this life without some pain and loss. If someone is mean to you, it probably comes from the fact that they are carrying their own pain. We are not going to get out of this alive so don't sweat the small stuff. Don't think about life too hard. It's mostly out of our control anyway. It took me a lifetime to get to this point and it's something I'm still working on. Now I just take one day at a time and try to find the good in things and in the people around me. Treat your life as I do now, like a long scenic drive. Did you ever get in the car and drive

The Lonely Boy

somewhere far away? You arrived safely and on time but you couldn't really remember how you got there. It's like being on automatic pilot. That's how I try to treat my life now. I just follow these simple rules of the road. They are as follows: pay attention, be courteous to others around you, and above all, just enjoy the ride. That's my mantra now. I am not totally healed yet, but I am on my way. I have learned after a lifetime of lessons to no longer be that lost and lonely boy.